Dream Manifestation Live Your Dreams

Dreams DO Come True

Dr. Jolene E. Church

Darlene Trujillo-Elliot

ISBN:0578422727
ISBN-13:978-0578422725

DREAM MANIFESTATION
LIVE YOUR DREAMS:
DREAMS DO COME TRUE

To order this and other Successful Thinking Mindset titles, please visit:

www.successfulthinkingmindset.com

Printed in North Charleston, SC 29406

USA

Library of Congress Cataloguing -in-Publication Data
Church, Jolene; Trujillo-Elliot, Darlene
Dream Manifestation Live Your Dreams: Dreams DO Come True
ISBN: 978-0578422725

Library of Congress Control Number: 2018912684

DEDICATION

To my husband Walter, children Ryan and lil Walter, my grandchildren Laya and Ryan, thank you for letting me be me and loving me with all my quirks. To Laya, your birth has given my life so much focus, clarity and courage. You have given me the courage to be front and center of my own life story. – *Darlene Trujillo-Elliot.*

To my children, Patrick, Kortnee, Ashlee, and Whitney, my grandchildren, Kaylee, Aiden, Brenten, Athena, and Sage. My life has been an inspired journey, inspired by my love for you and how each and every one of our dreams contributes to a better and more beautiful world. Live your dreams my loves – Live your inspired journey. – *Dr. Jolene Church*

Don’t call it a dream – call it a plan!

CONTENTS

Introduction 1

Dreams Exist 4

Exploring the Human Consciousness 25

Exploring the Spiritual Realm 41

Cultivating Your Desires 53

Pipe Dream or Reality? What's the Difference? 67

Making Your Mark- A Great Big World 81

When Our Dreams Seem Crushed 95

Believing/Accepting 111

Affirmation 127

Your Action Plan 145

Never stop believing in your dreams.

INTRODUCTION

On August 28th, 1963, Martin Luther King Jr. boldly stated in a public address, "I have a dream." Two years later in 1965, Sir Paul McCartney awoke from a vividly detailed dream of a song, fully formed- the song became the hit, *Yesterday*. Whether asleep or awake, our dreams are a part of our thoughts, a part of us. What many don't realize or fully understand is the role our dreams can play in the manifestation of the life we desire.

Aristotle stated that "We are what we repeatedly do." But we offer, that what we do, begins with what we think, and what we dream. Dreams do come true; we just need to know how to manifest our thoughts into action. We can imagine things that are not real. The song, *Yesterday*, was not real, but it became so. Martin Luther King Jr.'s dream was put into action, and mankind has been all the better for it.

Philosophers have argued for centuries over the existence of our thoughts, within the human consciousness or within the physical world- or do the two co-exist or collide? The Boomerang Effect in the world of social psychology is a set of unintended outcomes from an attempt to persuade, resulting in the adaptation of an opposing force instead. We would like to provide a philosophically opposing argument proposing that a force thrown that will come back, does not change, but returns the same.

Dream Manifestation Live Your Dreams: Dreams DO Come True is a philosophical and metaphysical exploration into casting out into the universe the very thing that you wish to receive back. Your dreams exist; you have created them. Therefore, the only thing left is the action of manifestation- doing. Let's do this together, let's explore what you want, what you desire, what you dream of, and find the place that where dreams meet reality.

For whatever you can believe- you can achieve.

1 DREAMS EXIST

What is it that you want? What have your longed for and desired? During the course of our lives we have many dreams and desires. They come they go, like the tides upon a sandy beach. Some dreams seem so vivid that they're like something that we could just reach out and grab. Others are harder to wrap your head around. Why is that? Why is it that it is harder to conceptualize and visualize ourselves living out specific dreams, whereas others we can *feel*? The answer to that likely is part of the reason that you picked up this book. It's intriguing to think, what if everything I dreamed of came true? Yet, how many times have you wished for something or longed for something, only later to say, "Thank God that didn't come to fruition!"

The power that we have over our dreams and the manifestation of them is quite remarkable and the power that we each have within us, that throttles down some of our dreams, can serve as both a safeguard and a detriment. Learning to harness that power, operate within our own power, and have control over our destiny is the purpose of this book.

For centuries people have explored the world of dreams, attempting to decipher and interpret the images and movies that play during our sleep. The ancient Greeks and Egyptians believed that during slumber, dreaming was some sort of supernatural messaging. Dream interpreters have been noted back to 3000-4000 B.C. and were considered divinely gifted message decipherers. In many societies, the distinction between slumber dreams and an awakened state were non-existent, as these societies chose to see dreams while asleep as an awakening of the soul for the advancement of the person while awake.

From Biblical times to Greek and Roman eras, dream interpretation was seen as a way to tap into universal information, knowledge and even an early warning system. Aristotle believed that dreams could be used as a physiological condition assessment tool whereas Freud saw dreams as a time when one's inhibitions, fears and ego are set aside, allowing the power of the unconscious mind to move forward and intercept our conscious state.

The Native Americans, Mexican, and Chinese cultures believe that dreams are a dimension wherein the unconscious and subconscious meet. Conversely, from the Middle Ages and into modern times, some religious groups have viewed dream interpretation as an evil act, condemning any foretelling of the future or predicting of physiological or physical events as satanic in nature.

This book is written from the viewpoint that embraces that of centuries of believers that our unconscious mind holds a power beyond what we think we know, but as we explore what we do know about the unconscious mind, we begin to demystify the world of dreams- both unconscious and awake. It is a shared belief of these authors that it is the power of the unconscious mind that awakens our consciousness and therefore puts us into our God-given right- freewill and choice. Is there a difference between what we dream in our sleep and what we dream or desire when awake? The simple answer is no.

What Are Dreams?

What are dreams? Are dreams real? Do dreams come true? These are age old questions and questions that many people continue to struggle with.

To put it simply, dreams are reminders from our unconscious that there are no limits. They are manifestations of the beautiful existence that we are a part of. They serve to warn us and inspire us. When tuned in, they are indeed the source of our human superpowers. We are superhuman- every last one of us- but only when we choose to be.

Dreams continually come to us during slumber as well as when we are wide awake. A dream can transport us, if even for a fleeting moment, into a new realm; a realm that exists. The physical reaction to our dreams is real. When you awaken from a joyous, happy dream, you feel happy. When you awaken from a nightmare, your heart pounds; so, we know a connection exists between the mind's perception of images, whether playing out as a movie during our sleep or a true physical experience during our awakened hours. We can see the manifestation of events in our minds, feel the emotions, and produce physical reactions, so the real question is, how do we get our dreams to a tangible state of *living the dream*? How do we go from driving a Ferrari in Monte Carlo in our dreams to driving a Ferrari in Monte Carlo during our awakened state?

There is a straightforward answer to this question. However, as our minds have become conditioned throughout our lives, a straightforward answer is not always accepted. This is where logic comes into play, as well as critical thinking. Our epistemic journey, how we receive information and assimilate that information into knowledge and beliefs, is through a series of activities. So rather than simply the straightforward answer, believe in your dreams and you will indeed live your dreams, a deeper explanation is required to help you fully assimilate this concept and build your belief system based on what makes sense to you.

As we grow into adulthood, we begin to place limits on our abilities and what we think we deserve, believing it's selfish to go after our dreams. If you can remember back to when you were a child, to a time when there were no boundaries, you couldn't comprehend when an adult told you that your dreams weren't possible. Having raised my children in the same manner, there were many arguments because they couldn't understand why their dreams were impossible. If you have a child, or have raised a child, you have likely used the incredibly intellectual reply, "Just because." And the standard reply from their little sweet voices is usually, "But, WHY?"

As parents we feel it is an important life lesson to teach our children about the boundaries and fears of this world. WE guide them and challenge their dreams, shaping them for them, into what we believe is acceptable and reasonable. We do this in the hopes to have an influence over the shaping of their dreams and their future into something that is *realistic*. This is not a new phenomenon. This is how we were raised, and a perpetual cycle of dream censoring as we raise our children.

As parents, we feel that it is our responsibility to make sure that our children are protected within the sanctity of *reality*. We try our best to provide the *picket fence life*, free of weeds, and thorns, and heaven forbid we imagine a yard without a fence! But we have got it all wrong.

Dreams are sacred. They are gifts from God to help us grow our souls and make the best of our physical environment. They help us push past limitations that our physical world put on us. Why not defy the laws of *what is reality*?! Dreams are meant to motivate, to help us be our personal best and reach amazing potential that we may not even be aware that we have. Dreams exist within us, just awaiting their birth. We are pregnant with dreams throughout our existence and created to have a multitude of births throughout our lives.

Everyone has their own dreams. These are custom creations that have been made especially for them, and by them. Dreams help us remain excited about the possibilities of life. Why would we want to try to survive any other way? Imagine a life without dreams- it's preposterous! How could we live without dreams? We can't, and that is why dreams are as important as the air we breathe. Dreams exist so that we can live. We live because we dream, and dreams are alive because we exist and breathe life into our dreams.

Just as every sunset and sunrise have been designed especially for you, so have your dreams, because you are the creator of your dreams, just as you are the creator of every sunrise and sunset. How can this be so? Think of a sky full of fluffy white clouds gently flowing across the sky. What do you see in the clouds? You may see an elephant, a face, or a tree. The imaginary shapes that float across the sky are what you create in your mind, from what you see. We can even point out the shapes and share this experience with others. What you perceive and shape within your mind becomes the experience of another person. We become co-creators of reality, of experience.

We cannot argue that the elephant is not real, as within your mind, the cloud took on a shape, which was an elephant. It may not be the same elephant at the zoo eating hay, but it is what you perceived it and made it to be. The same is true for our sunsets and sunrises. When you see the beautiful purple and orange of the sun slowly sinking into the horizon, the beauty that you embrace and how you perceive it is your lived experience. Nobody else sees exactly the same thing. Your mind sends you messages of perception, such as how the sunset makes you feel. Within your mind, thoughts from what you see, and feel are melded together. Once again, you can express to others what you see and share the experience, but it is still your creation. And to the other person it is theirs.

When we dream, much like when we imagine, we shape what we see through what we feel and see within our mind. Unlike the sunset, the picture is within, rather than in our external environment. Sometimes it is a picture-less thought. Other times it is a vivid cinematic experience of the mind. We can close our eyes and feel like we are there. That is because we are. Dreams are not unreal, and reality is the only thing real, for what is reality? What is real? What is unreal? Is there such a thing?

Dreams exist, because we create them. Once created, they exist. They do not disappear, although they can be suppressed, buried, or hidden. We can ignore them, others can try to crush them, yet they still exist. Existence is infinite. That means our dreams live on forever, but as we well know, we can go through life living or we can go through life simply existing. Wouldn't you rather your dreams live? And that you live your dream life? Why would we want our dreams to simply exist and not be lived? Preposterous, right?

So how do we live our dreams? How do we breathe life into our dreams? The key is to understand that whether you decide to act on your dream, it exists. It won't die, but you need your dreams to truly live. So, who or what really dies?

Imagination- Your Dream Machine

People often ask me, what is the difference between imagination and dreams? Are they one in the same? My answer is simple: imagination is the engine of our dreams. It acts as the heart and lungs do for the body. It is the generation system, that when activated, produces life. Our dreams provide us with life giving energy. For every dream, our heart beats and our lungs expand with air.

Our imagination is the initial creation device. What we can conceptualize within our mind, we can then connect to and turn it into a dream. A dream is the result of our imagination. A dream is at the axis of where what we think, and what we feel, unite. Once imagined and connected, our dreams become reality. They have shape, just as the clouds in the sky. You can see it. You can feel it. You can connect what is in your head with your senses, some immediately, others may take time.

Think of something you have dreamed of. Finding that perfect life partner, winning the lottery, going on a trip to an exotic place. Whatever your dream, it lives, it exists within you. It exists because you thought of it and created it. You can see it, right? Okay, the picture exists. Let's connect a bit more to this dream of yours. Imagine, yep- go into creation mode- how having what you dream of would make you feel. Imagine yourself in that place. In the arms of your love, going on a shopping spree, or relaxing in the cottage courtyard of a quaint village in Ireland. Imagine yourself living your dream. Think of how you feel. Think of your emotional state. Feel your skin.

Imagine your every sensation. Smell, sights, sound, touch, and taste.

If in your vision of your little Irish cottage you have a lovely breakfast set before you in the garden; what does it smell like? What do those potatoes taste like? Are there birds chirping around you? Or do you hear the wind rustling through the grass? Can you feel the temperature of the air? Are you chilly? Warm?

Connecting what you dream of with your senses, helps you fully form your dream. Think of it as an inflatable balloon at the Macy's Thanksgiving Day parade. At first, it is just a big shape. Once the balloon begins to be inflated, it starts to take shape. Filling the balloon full makes it so that you and others can recognize it for what it is. Until then, it has shape, but until full, it cannot soar through the air in a shape that others would fully recognize and appreciate. As you imagine and connect to your dreams, others will take notice. They can't help it!

It is the connection with your dream that brings your dream to life, which helps you work toward fruition and manifestation of living your dream. Dreams have an amazing sense of energy. The motivational component of dreams is a life-giving energy. Without dreams, we merely exist. Therefore, imagination is a core function of living.

Whether or not you care for Disneyland, one cannot help but be amazed at the level of imagination that was the creative engine behind Walt Disney's dream. The entire park is a living dream. It is the result of an imagined thought, connected to senses, and brought to life. We can experience someone else's dream. We live as a part of someone else's dream. What's really cool is that as we imagine within the dream, we are creating new dreams. This is the infinite nature of dreams.

We dream and create. We experience someone else's dream, we expand their dream and likely have thoughts of our own that expand the dream. Every time you said the words, "I wish I…." you have started the dream process. You have imagined and therefore birthed a new dream. Will you breathe life into it? It exists, so why let it just lay there. Your dreams aren't meant to be couch potatoes. Exercise them. Get their lungs pumping. Get that heart rate up. Once you have given birth to the dream, it is now up to you to nurture it. It's not going away. It will still be there. Do something!

Perhaps you want a better life or just something in your life that you desire. If you have imagined what it is that you desire, then why aren't you doing something about it? If you never act, you will never have it. It all starts with the recognition of the existence of your dream. There are no excuses in dream land, only breathing. There is only positive energy- belief.

If you do not start living, you will atrophy. We need dreams. We need their energy. We need their driving force. We need their optimism and hope. We need to push beyond what we see in the physical world and connect what we see in our heads. We can connect the two. Many before you and I have done it and many more after us will as well. We can choose to excuse away our dream atrophy or we can build our dream muscle.

What do you want? What is the dream that you strongly desire? Why can't you have it? If you have a reason, this is the first challenge.

You need to get re-creating what can and cannot be. Your imagination is the key. You must create how you can. You must create that you already have it. You must put yourself right into the moment of realizing that you have created a dream that is waiting to live. And you are waiting to live your dream. The co-existence of you and your dream are inseparable. You are married to your dream. Will you be faithful? No matter how long it may take and how frustrated you may become? You must commit. If you are afraid of commitment, then you are going to need to address that; challenge #2! You must have an undying and unwavering belief and commitment to your dreams for them to manifest into the physical world.

There are so many beautiful dreams inside of you just waiting to be born. This is your life, your story, all you have to do is seize it.

Often times we get so stuck in the details of our everyday life, that we just don't look up to see what's going on. Have you ever thought about your life-story being told as a movie? What does it look like? Is it happy? Does it end in sadness?? Does it inspire? How does it make you feel? Would you recognize yourself in your own movie?

The hustle and bustle of everyday life, errands and busy schedules, hold us hostage from our own happiness. It's time to rewrite the story. It's time to abandon the labels that we have put on ourselves and that we have allowed others to define us. It's time to let go of current definitions. The mother, the father, the lawyer, the student, whatever your current label, it's time to let it go. It's not always comfortable letting go. Letting go of what has defined us may leave us feeling like there is a pit or a void. There may be a feeling of abandonment.

Play your movie again in your head and replay it with a different story line, with different labels, and different expectations. Imagine when you take all the complications of life away, when you allow the labels to dissipate, fear somehow just melts away. Thinking to your original life movie, would you make the same decisions as you originally did? Would you take the same path, or would you try something different? When you start from a fresh perspective, that you have nothing to lose, your life movie changes from black and white to a high-definition explosion of color and sensations.

Our life movie will always have a beginning and an end, but what is the story that plays out in between the opening and closing credits? Did you play a part in writing it? Or did you let the circumstances of life dictate which path you chose? Did the plot just unwind and you found yourself jumping into whichever role was needed? We can't live like this. We need to stop and recognize where we are and what we truly desire. It is only then, that we watch our movie start to take on a new direction. It is only then, that we understand that our dreams can't catch us if we are in a state of reaction instead of creation. Our current circumstances do not dictate our destination.

How many people have you known (or maybe it's you?) that have been held back by what happened in the past? Had this or that not happened then I could have… If I'd have gone to school…. If I wouldn't have… Don't get stuck in the movie *Groundhogs Day*! Just like Bill Murray figured out in the movie after repeating the same day over and over and trying to manipulate the vicious cycle through a series of insincere acts, our movie will remain on repeat if we do nothing, in true sincerity and consciousness, to change it. Our movie cannot change if we blame others or our circumstances. Those things are unimportant. I know a young man that slept in a tent for two years so that he would not be bogged down by expenses because he wanted his dream so bad.

Excuses are just repeat mechanisms in our life movie. Our movie will keep looping and our dreams will simply exist in a superficial state, with no lifeblood or breath. We must focus on the dream, not our current state to break the repeat cycle.

It's important that you know your dreams are waiting for you and will continue to wait, until you are ready to receive. One of the things that we condition ourselves to believe is that dream achievement means sacrifice. Not only does this cast a negative light on our dreams and potential, but this half-truth may actually inhibit us from truly dreaming or much worse, to even try. Even though my friend *sacrificed* a warm bed and the creature comforts of a home by sleeping in a tent for two years, there was nothing sacrificial about it. What he saw was that there was a barrier between his dream and the physical world that he could eliminate. By not having rent, he had the additional resources to inch closer to what he desired. By eliminating excuses, he took himself out of the repeat cycle of his movie and began living the new reality that he had created. He began living his dream.

The Real Boomerang Effect

Everything in life is energy. It is unlikely that you have not heard of yin and yang. The feminine and masculine interaction of dark and light and good and evil. It is the balance of the universe, what scientists and physicists have explained as equally opposing forces and the great equalizer. It is like a boomerang where what is thrown, returns. What you put forth into the universe, will come back to you. We call this the *Real Boomerang Effect*. Why *real*?

In social psychology, another boomerang effect theory exists. The theory postulates that unintended consequences are achieved when a person attempts to persuade another of an opposing viewpoint and the persuader then instead adopts the opposing viewpoint. The theory is based on a fear of anti-conformity and actually supports our theory that a natural part of the universe is to create and co-create dreams. When we do not infringe on the freedom of others by burdening them with our desires, there is no resistance. By putting out into the universe what we desire, the reverberation can only be that of what has been cast; therefore, we boomerang back to us what we have cast.

Everyone born on this earth is here to play an active part in the creation of their life movie. Life is not a spectator sport; at least not if you want to live your dreams. Your dreams exist, it's time to live them. It's time to move from reaction to creation. It's time to stop blaming or relying on others. Your dreams belong to you; own them; live them.

The moment you stop to think about what is really important to you, to your core, what you truly desire, is the moment you begin to create. But should we have everything that we dream up? There is creativity, just imagining new things and then there is true dreaming. Each provides pictures to the mind. Each breaths life and existence into something new, but one is driven by something deeper. There is a calling deep within each one of us that one day we will live our dream path.

How do you know when you are on your dream path? Your dream path is distinctively recognizable as doors will open that you didn't even know existed. The universe will begin to prepare you for the life you were supposed to be working towards.

Take a leap of faith. Abandon the labels. Say yes to your dreams. Say yes to the challenges of your dreams.

Believing in Your Dreams Again

Everyone on this earth is here for a reason, to live out our dreams. But how do we get back to that childhood state of dreaming without restrictions? The answer: simply by learning to begin to realize what makes us truly happy.

A true desire is a fiery, passionate and focused awareness that calls out to the universe. When you dream vividly it is like a burning desire, all that you can think about. It can make you feel like you are about to explode with excitement, a feeling of *I can't wait* and anticipation. That fire, anticipation, and excitement is your dream, in the birth canal, and you are in labor.

What is it that you long for? What is it that can hold your attention for a long time? This isn't the time to sell yourself short or to tell yourself that you only deserve a small portion- dream in big, in proportion to the vastness of the universe! You must realize that there is not a limit to what you can have. When we start looking at the world around us through a restrictive lens, like there is not enough to go around, we limit the power within us.

In defining what you truly desire, you must be focused. If you are vague in your objectives, you will get vague results. If you don't know what you want, then it's time to work on your dream muscles. The subconscious only works when you can hold your own attention. This is no time for conscious attention deficit disorder (CADD). Focus births dreams. In Lamaze class, pregnant women and their partners learn the power of focused breathing to relieve the tensions that oppose the natural childbirth. Focus toward our dreams has the same relaxing and opposition clearing effect of Lamaze. Breath- your dreams are waiting to be born. Believe you have the power to make this happen.

We say, believe in your dreams, AGAIN- as if you had once believed and now do not. This is a somewhat over-simplified generalization, but what happens through life experiences is a dilution of our ability to dream. When we are children we not only have the ability to pretend and fantasize, but to manifest what we desire- we make dreams come true. There is an innocence in our youth that enables us to connect with what we want- the key to bringing dreams to life.

I'm going to ask you again, what do you want? What do you truly want? What is really great about dreams is that as you think, reflect, and desire, you have already put your dream into action. What will you do next? This is key, as many dreams become like zombies, existing with no direction or lifeblood.

As any parent, not faced with fertility issues can attest, making the baby is the easy part, and fun! Creation is natural to the universe. The beginning of life is a stunning and miraculous event, but it doesn't stop at creation; just ask the parents of a 3-year-old throwing a tantrum on the floor of the grocery store. Creation is followed by continual action. Your dreams require a state of continual motion.

Some believe that it is enough to cast your desire to the universe, sit back with a bag of chips, and await your deepest desires to appear. I hate to burst your bubble, but sitting with a bag of chips is an action, but not the action that is going to provide you with the fulfillment of your dreams- unless your dream is to be sitting day after day with a bag of chips and an oversized gut.

When I was a kid, I dreamed of being a veterinarian, among many other occupations. My mom would drop me off at the library and I would scour the shelves for book after book on animals. I wanted to know as much as I could. I didn't know that I was actually, fueling a dream. With every new book and every page that I read, I was setting into motion a dream. The more I learned, the more I dedicated myself to the thought that becoming a veterinarian was the ideal career path for me. So why did I not become a veterinarian? The answer is linked to our natural ability to dream as a child. This is something we may lose as we experience life.

Kids dream and dream often. For children, dreams change without guilt. As adults, we tend to cast judgment on ourselves and others when we jump from dream to dream. Why can't our dreams shape shift? Just as our interests transformed, grew, shifted, and changed during our childhood, so too do our dreams. There are some people that feel the calling from a newly created dream and never let go. You can recognize these folks by their undying commitment from a young age to the achievement and fulfillment of a specific dream.

Why didn't I become a veterinarian? I dream-shifted. What was a dream and an interest, led to an evolution of my dream to something new, driven by passion. What's interesting was that I still pursued a path toward becoming a doctor- eventually. What's beautiful about dream-shifting is that we stay in a perpetual state of creation. This is something that I have never lost, but unfortunately I know many that have. They don't forget how to dream, per se, but they forget how to believe.

A terrible habit of adults is guilt. We are so hard on ourselves, and we need to let this go. It is what kills creation and stops our birthing process- what we have been put on earth to do- reproduce. If you come from a Christian belief system, you may remember in Genesis 1:28 that God commanded Adam and Eve to be fruitful and multiply and replenish the earth. He gave them dominion over every living thing; including what holds us back.

We need to learn how to stop holding ourselves back and limiting ourselves. Guilt is a form of judgment. Judgment comes from external influences in our environment. It is the result of experiences. Think about that. When you were three, do you remember thinking about the size of your thighs? Of course not. As we live and experience life, while interacting with others, we experience judgment. Unfortunately, we begin to measure ourselves against others and can become our own worst enemy. So how are dreams affected by judgment?

As children it's natural to dream of being an astronaut, followed by a fireman, and then perhaps a jockey. Our dreaming is not inhibited by judgment. It's okay to dream-shift and transform one dream into a new one. Rather than abandoning the original dream, we naturally transition our passion to a new dream.

Dream-shifting as an adult is met with not only self-judgment, but the judgment of others. How so? Think about it. If you tell your family, "I would like to start a bumper sticker business," and then as you develop your knowledge and interest, you suddenly realize that something else really fuels you; your family may consider you flighty.

For years, following the original Mission Impossible movie, twelve years to be exact, I dreamed of owning an Audi TT. When I finally got behind of the wheel of the car I had dreamed of owning for so long, I decided that I no longer wanted to experience my Audi TT dream- so I shifted the dream. Some could judge and make assumptions that I truly didn't know what I wanted or perhaps I allowed bias or circumstances (I had a terrible test drive) to derail my dream, but none of that matters. What does matter is that I didn't just simply abandon my dream, I shifted my belief into a new dream and desire- and I'm okay with that. And to be able to remain in a state of creation, the most important part of dream manifestation, we must be okay with letting go. When we let go of any guilt and judgment, we are open to dream and create. When we can do this, we allow ourselves to believe in ourselves and in our dreams.

When we can accept that sometimes what we desire changes, we free ourselves to shift to a new belief. We must believe to receive. What we believe comes back to us. We get so bound up and limited as we experience guilt for not *following through* with a dream that we stop believing that we can have or achieve anything. We judge ourselves into a state of disbelief.

Our dreams exist because we create them. As soon as you dream it, it becomes as real as if you were touching it, living it, experiencing it. Belief is the breath of your dreams. Breathe and believe. Fuel the fire and add air by breathing. Your passion can burn bright- as bright as you allow it to burn. Your dreams can become more and more tangible, if you just keep breathing- keep the motion of life going. Creation isn't meant to be dormant, but alive and breathing.

Dream-shifting is a simple transfer of life energy as your passion and desires change- welcome the shift- welcome the continual flow of energy as your dreams evolve into something new. Don't label yourself a quitter or not good enough. Don't judge that you don't have what it takes or the resources to achieve your dream. Abandon the labels and get rid of your guilt-ridden baggage- it is time for you to believe in your dreams again. It is time to believe that you can and will achieve your dreams. Are you ready?

2 EXPLORING THE HUMAN CONSCIOUSNESS

She felt a ting of excitement in her stomach as she walked toward the podium. Her heart swelled with pride as she realized that what she had worked so hard for and dreamed of for so long had come to fruition. As her right hand was tightly grasped by another in a solemn congratulatory handshake and her other hand gripped the diploma, she realized, "I did it." Her dream had come true. The ting of excitement was not just a feeling, but instead a stirring of the inner consciousness; it is the driving force within each and every one of us.

The question of what exactly the human consciousness has been at the heart of much scientific debate for many moons. What exactly is that *thing* inside us that makes us tick and provides us with our joy, knowledge, and drive? Where is our human consciousness? Does it occupy space?

The premise of the 2003 movie, 21 Grams was based on a 1907 scientific study wherein physician Duncan MacDougall postulated that the soul could be measured. MacDougal theorized that soul had weight and attempted to measure any difference in mass body weight at the point of death when the soul departed the body. Although the experiment was deemed flawed and unscientific by the research community due to the small sample size and that only one of the six subjects met the hypothesis, the concept of the existence of a soul is still widely accepted across many groups of people.

When we become aware of our soul, this core component within each of us that we don't quite always understand how to reach, we have tapped through into consciousness. There is great power in this place. The fascination with its proven power has intrigued scientists for centuries.

Hard science is based on observations and measurements, so how then can what has been thought of as a metaphysical aspect of our being be explained and understood? To take the mystery out of human consciousness, in 2014, MIT scientist Max Tegmark, provided a theory that the human consciousness is a state of matter, known as quanta. This means that like other matter, whether liquid, gas, or solid, quanta can be measured, and it is governed by the same laws of physics as the rest of the universe. Tegmark's research essentially likens the human consciousness to a vast computer database; one that is capable of storing and retrieving massive amounts of information.

When we become aware and tuned-in to our consciousness, our perceptions are heightened, and we operate from a superior position of strength. The reason for this follows the laws of physics. Primarily, if we look at Newton's Law of Motion, the law on inertia, we can gain insight into how our consciousness influences our ability to manifest what we desire as well as attract that which we do not want. The law states that an object continues in its state of rest or of uniform motion unless compelled to change that state by an external force.

When we apply this law to our dreams and desires, it is easy to see that when we turn on our dream engine, how we can then move forward toward the manifestation of that dream. When we tell ourselves, internalize to our subconscious, what we desire, we fuel an internal fire. Once internalized, this new *information*, our desire, becomes a part of the framework and database of our consciousness quanta, a realm of creation. Why does this matter?

What we internalize isn't always what we want to internalize. We are told that we are too short, not clever enough, or that we don't have the resources to do something that we desire. Those messages become a part of our consciousness. It takes a purposive connection with our consciousness to push past any negative information to clear the path for a positive energy flow to manifest what we want.

Deliberately feeding our consciousness with what we want and then connecting with your inner consciousness by *checking in*, enables you to *manage your data flow*. Have you ever heard the phrase "garbage in, garbage out?" Whatever we feed our mind and human consciousness, we emit. Feed dreams and desires in, and receive dreams and desires out- but this is not automatic.

Imagine turning on your computer, typing in a bunch of information and then sitting back and expecting the computer to just randomly produce a brilliant piece of work. That's not how it works. Your computer can produce that brilliant piece of work, but steps may need to be followed to get there. Additional information, which is written in the code of various programs on your computer will help in completing the steps in those tasks. Your consciousness is the same.

The quantum matter that binds together the knowledge within you with what you experience can be influenced to shift what you physically experience. Just like the law of inertia, when we move thoughts, which are pictures in the mind, we move and change the world as we see it. For example, if you imagine yourself (see a picture in your mind) of something that has not happened, with ongoing connection between what is and what has yet to come, the mind works with the law of inertia, moving in the direction of what you desire. This can happen both to your benefit and detriment, so tuning-in to your consciousness through awareness is imperative to receiving that which you want to receive and not what you do not. What ball are you sending into motion with your thought?

What You Don't Know You Know

Sometimes we *feel* like we should do something, that we should check question *a.* rather than questions *b.* or *c.* on a test. We *just know* that we should take that job or start that conversation. We can't explain it.

So many times, in so many conversations, we hear reference to a *gut feeling* or *I just knew*. But how do we *just know*? and what is our *gut*? The human consciousness is a miraculous energy. The quantum energy is continually in motion. Some might call it a machine that churns out *dream fixins*. When we look at our consciousness through an exploration of philosophy, we gain a greater appreciation for how important it is to have a heightened level of awareness in consciousness.

French philosopher René Descartes introduced mankind to an amazing world of the human consciousness. His philosophy, "I think therefore I am," has been argued feverishly for centuries, for where does knowledge originate? Descartes argued that there are many absolutes and in absolute knowledge, there is no argument.

I think, therefore I exist, indicates that if my mind is such that I have knowledge to think and understand, then the realization that an absolute exists- I exist- cannot be countered. *Apriori* knowledge- knowledge known before instruction- inborn knowledge creates a duality of mind and body. We cannot, therefore, believe or realize our own existence without prior thinking capability. So where does this knowledge come from?

There is a school of thought that believes that our minds retain information that was a part of our experience from the time that we were conceived. This means that from the time the energy of our cells began to multiply into the beautiful beings that we have become, everything in our environment becomes a part of our experience. This explains how some children have a *knack at* a hobby, profession, or craft similar to that of a family member, even if that family member has passed and the individual had little exposure to this person. Sounds of the world and conversations become a part of an unborn experience. Later in life that adult may have some *strange recollection* or *knowing* that they cannot explain.

Yet another school of thought maintains that we are beings that possess absolute knowledge of the universe and beyond. This comes from our connected energy, from which we are all sourced. We have power and knowledge locked away within us that we simply need keys to unlock. Keys can be acquired through looking deep within. It has been said that much of the right side of the brain can be tapped by engaging the left.

The right side of the brain is the side that creativity resides. We perform tasks, such as habits, from this side of the brain. The right-brain is responsible for 3-D thinking, for imagination, intuition, and insight. Music and creativity light up the senses within this side of the brain.

The left side is our logical side. This is the side that mathematics and science rule. The analytical left-brain is where numbers and language are subject to reasoning and logical thought processing. Imagine your entire brain infused with quantum processors-recording for playback your every bit of knowledge, thought and experience.

In our daily lives we are forced to think from the left side of our brain. We must make decisions and perform calculations on a daily basis. Some believe that because our left-brain gets so much of a workout that the power available to us is left virtually untapped in the right-brain. By working out the right-brain we can manifest things into our lives that would make no sense to the left; it would be illogical. The thinking is that if we can engage more of our brain through deliberate exercising of the right-brain, we can tap into not only unseen knowledge, but rapidly access the absolute knowledge within.

Have you taken a multiple-choice test and changed your initial answer, only later to realize that you were right in the first place and the answer that you changed to was wrong? This is because the left brain can be a dirty little trickster as the logic side analyzes and questions your *own knowing.* In dream manifestation, this *trickster* can be a dream-killer.

Let's go back to the discussion on our subconscious thoughts while we are in an *unconscious state.* What's interesting is that during our sleep we may be at our highest state of consciousness, but as discussed, the left and right side of our brains have different priorities. When in an auto-pilot state, sleep, the ego and bias don't exist, but what's fascinating is that what you have unconsciously fed into your subconscious is awakened.

Fall asleep after watching a disturbing movie or simply while watching the nightly news and you may very well have images within your dreams of these shows. Find yourself worried over your ability to perform a task at work and you may find yourself in some sort of turmoil or trouble in your dream-state. We are not only exposed to external images and ideas throughout the day, but we also are exposed to our own doubts, fears, and inhibitions. Oftentimes these are suppressed, and we don't even fully realize that we are experiencing these things at all. Throw enough garbage in the pail and eventually it will get full and overflow.

Fear of what we don't know can be crippling. Fearful thoughts are an opposing force which buries itself into the mind and only pops up as we attempt to move in the opposite direction. These thoughts become deep-seated beliefs that are like massive linebackers in your head. They block creative thinking and new information through a shield of fear and uncertainty.

Connecting our sleeping dream state to our awakened state and achieving a higher level of consciousness may not happen overnight, but who knows, it may. Does it really matter how long it takes, as long as it happens?

When we are asleep, our mind is processing and working through problems. It is a puzzle master, looking for solutions, uncovering clues, and providing insightful information, but we must be open and in tune enough to send and receive in this state. Yes, you heard that right, send and receive. You have the power to consciously feed what you want played out in your dreams while you sleep. When you can influence your unconscious mind, you can connect with your subconscious. Much of what we don't realize we know resides there and our influence upon our subconscious can help us manifest fruitful actions in our conscious state.

What we know and what we do not know resides in the same place. What we choose to give more significance to becomes the ruler of how we believe, what we see, and what we achieve. As we provide influence on our subconscious for the state that we would like to be in, the subconscious discerns no difference between what is and what is to be.

An awareness of our ability to influence the subconscious, and an understanding of what control we have to tap into this, puts us into a higher state of awareness and consciousness. A higher state of consciousness is one that puts us beyond what we know and don't know, to a state of being, the state of *I am*.

I am is a powerful state, a state wherein anything is possible. Although the logical side of the brain will quickly jump in and say, "but you aren't," this doesn't mean that *I am* does not exist. *I am* exists whether you believe it or not, or whether you know or not; *I am* just is. What does this mean?

I am is a transformative statement that instantly transforms the proclaimer into a virtual state of being. Christians believe that we are children of God, created in His image, and that He is the *Great I Am*. Think about this for a minute. If we are children of God and created in His image, our potential has been described and prescribed by God. We must allow ourselves to reside in the state that we were destined to be and created in- *I am*.

Separate yourself from any religious context of that, yet believe that you were created in an image of all-knowing, all-seeing, and all-being. *I can't* simply isn't possible for a being created in an image of all-encompassing power.

From the state of *I am* we can get to the place that we desire to be and have the things in our life that we desire. The power to unlock our knowledge and the power to unlock our potential comes from a state of *I am*. From this state of higher thinking we tap into the creative energy generator of the right-brain that connects the *doing side* of the brain with the necessary actions to create results.

A Higher Calling

Our consciousness is as vital to our health as our circulatory and immune system, and many holistic healers believe that it actually supports the physical health of these systems. Our consciousness contributes to a clearer, more focused, and healthy state of mental health. So, what exactly is consciousness?

Consciousness is a state of awareness and awakening. When you awake from your sleep, you awaken into a physical state of consciousness; but are you mentally conscious? We often allow our auto-pilot mechanisms to take control from the moment we awake; to do this short-changes our potential. This is where our unconscious and our conscious can engage and magic can happen, but we need to truly have an awakening.

From time to time, most of us have been told to slow down or to take time to smell the roses. What is meant by this is that we need to stop and reclaim our consciousness. When you stop to smell the roses, you pause to engage in the world around you. You take in the sweet perfume of the rose and within your mind you decide whether it is pleasing or not. This experience cannot be done passively. You must physically stop, deliberately smell the rose, and consciously reflect within to determine what the effect of the rose has on you.

Our conscious state is where we have the most power. This is the state that we can find our purpose, find our calling, reach for our dreams, and realize joy. Joy is like the perfume of the rose, we must stop to experience it. In our state of consciousness, stopping to realize where we are, and awakening to how that makes us feel, gives us the most power. In a later chapter you will read how appreciation can enhance this power, but far before that state, we must pause and take in what we are thinking, believing, and desiring.

All too many people enter into a time of searching, known as a mid-life crisis. This is a time when a person believes that life has passed them by and that they missed an opportunity. For some, a shiny red sports car or surfing every day becomes an obsession. They believe that the car or activity will help them reclaim something that they believe was stolen from them. What they were truly missing out on was a state of joy achieved through consciousness; for within joy purpose can be found.

We weren't put on this planet to occupy space or collect dust. The saying ashes to ashes, dust to dust, derived from the English Burial Service and Genesis 3:19 KJV, indicates that from dust we are formed and to dust we shall return. Take this a bit deeper and think about this. We come from but a speck, that until it takes form, does not have the power to change the world. If we sit idle and collect dust, we accomplish no more than the one who has already returned to a speck within the ground. Our greater purpose is to be a rolling stone, to not sit idly, and never collect dust. How do we determine our direction? We accomplish that through joy.

Developing Your Joy

Joy gives us direction and provides dimension to our experience. Try this little joy exercise. The very best time to practice this exercise is when you first awake, but any comfortable place, free from distractions will do. You can even do this in your office, sitting in the parking lot in your car, or on a park bench. I like to do this when I wake up as it only takes a few minutes and helps me become conscious, joyful, and fire up my dream manifestation furnace.

In your comfortable, distraction-free space, close your eyes. Become aware of what is around you. If you are in bed, take notice of the feeling of the softness of the mattress or your pillow, how warm you are, how nice it feels. Focus only on the positive elements. If there are cockroaches crawling up your wall, loud traffic out the window, or screaming kids, tune them out for just the amount of time necessary to find a positive element. Only you have the power to move yourself to a state of joy so take the time to find it and to do so.

Joy can be illusive, the monotony and pressures of daily life, disappointments, and the negative energy of those around us can cause us to lose touch with our joy, but joy still exists. As you focus on the wonderful, positive sensations that you feel, embrace that feeling. Embrace that feeling and let it bring a smile to your face. Joy cannot be contained; it will manifest in your expression and actions.

From this state of joy, you are ripe to dream and think of what is important to you. Your consciousness of where you are and what is important to you will help you develop a joyful plan for your future. To some, they may want to be able to afford to buy food for the hungry, because they experienced hunger and know the pain associated. Others might want to travel the world so that they can share stories and knowledge with others.

Within each of our selfish desires is tied a joyful act. It is from practicing and developing your joy, focusing on the good smells, sounds, and other sensations in the moment, that your joy will get stronger. It is a manifestation of something within that cannot be contained. When it is cultivated and matured, you won't want to contain it. It will feel like a bubble in you about to burst and you just want to share the goodness from within with as many people around you.

Imagine yourself sitting on a park bench at lunch, away from the office. You close your eyes for a moment and feel the warm breeze, and hear the wind in the trees. You hear the birds and realize that you are in a serene place, even if you're in the middle of a big city. Serenity is where you find it. As you feel the positive energy of this place, think of something, that if you had the power to do to improve the life of others, you would do. Visualize yourself doing that thing. Let's pretend you see yourself winning the lottery and starting a non-profit providing shoes and clothes for the impoverished and food for the hungry. How does it make you feel? Imagine the smiling and grateful faces, faces relieved of pain and discomfort, knowing that you had something to do with that. Embrace that joy as you now shift to something that you greatly desire in your life. There are no limits. What is that thing? Feel it being a part of your life.

Just as you imagine the smile coming to the face of a needy person when they are provided with basic provisions that they did not know how they would receive, imagine that feeling for yourself. Imagine the feeling when you read off one matching lottery number after another. Imagine the feeling in your heart as you complete a lifelong dream. Visualize the smile on your face when you realize you accomplished something huge! Do you feel the feeling of joy inside as you imagine the huge smile on your face? What would it feel like to call your best friend or family member and share the good news with them? Would your heart beat fast? Could you dial the phone fast enough?

Wherever you are practicing this exercise, bed, park bench, or in your office, imagine yourself in this place closing your eyes and realizing that you have what you dream. How would this make you feel? Embrace that joy. Now imagine that you closed your eyes and realized that not only do you have what you always dreamed but that you also have done that great thing that would improve the life of others. Do you feel accomplished? Proud? Joyful? Claim it. In your mind state, "I am joyful. I am appreciative of what I desire, because that is what will be. I am in a joyful state of creation and manifestation of all that I desire. It is my destiny to succeed. I deserve this."

Repeat this exercise frequently. Finding joy and the associated purpose that brings joy will help you manifest bigger than life- bigger than left-brained logical dreams. Joy is as close as you allow it to be. Sometimes we need to look past some pretty ugly stuff to find it, but it is there. Claim it. Become conscious of what is good and what good you have inside; this will manifest into amazing things if you allow it.

Connecting Your Dreams

Centuries old beliefs that dreams are some sort of connective layer between unseen and seen worlds may not be so far-fetched. Premonitions through dreams, whether awake or asleep, may not be explained in ways that satisfy hard science experts, but for social scientists, the philosophical and psychological elements of dream or even premonition phenomenon don't seem so hard to comprehend. Similarly, there seems to be no difference between thoughts formed in sleeping dreams than thoughts formed in an awakened state, other than what part of the brain is driving- unconscious or conscious. Both, however have the same influence, subconscious thoughts.

In our sleeping state, the subconscious feeds the unconscious mind with anything that has been fed to it. Juxtapose our daydreams and we find the same underlying influence into whether we believe our dream is achievable or not, and that is the subconscious mind. Whether you think you can or think you can't, these are influences of your subconscious.

If you can fly in your sleeping dreams, what is the message from your subconscious mind? That's right, that you have no limitations. What if you are falling or stumbling and you just can't seem to move forward? Your subconscious is trying to communicate the barrier that is blocking you from achieving whatever it is that you desire. Of course, these are simplified dream interpretations but nonetheless illustrate just how important it is to pay attention to what is playing out in your subconscious mind. Even if you watch the Walking Dead before bed and have a zombie dream- you just might want to lay in bed when you wake up and give additional thought to that dream. I like to keep a dream journal.

By journaling my dreams, I am able to list details that I may not have paid much attention to, but when they are on paper they stick out like a sore thumb. Patterns of thoughts can be identified. If something is bugging you or your subconscious is actively trying to work out an issue in your unconscious mind, you will spot this when you journal.

Journaling helps identify what is going on in your subconscious. Although I find dream journaling extremely revealing, journaling one's thoughts at the end of the day is equally helpful in releasing pent up thoughts that you may not even be aware you are harboring. These might be frustrations or fears. Remember the Lamaze breathing; if we are tense, we are creating a field of resistance from our subconscious that will affect results manifestation in our conscious. Anything that we can do to increase our awareness will help us in reducing these resistance barriers.

3 EXPLORING THE SPIRITUAL REALM

To understand the Spiritual Realm, you first must acknowledge that our souls are one with the universal energy. Energy is everywhere; it exists where we cannot see it. Energy comes in different forms through heat (thermal), light (radiant), motion (kinetic), electrical, chemical and gravitational. If you look closely at all objects, they vibrate on an energetic level. It is all around us and it is a part of us. It is everywhere! And yet we still struggle to get our brains around it.

The reason energy is so hard to understand is because it's abstract and most of us, who are not scientists or engineers, are forced to have faith that it even exists. It stands to reason that if you are reading this book, you must have some sort of faith that the spiritual realm is here. Or maybe you are curious.

That's okay. This life is a learning experience and a time to explore. This means exploring both the seen and unseen, accomplished and never yet accomplished. This is the perfect time to explore the beauty of the spiritual realm that surrounds us and that we are a part of. For those of you who say pish posh to faith and to anything spiritual because it cannot be seen, let me provide you with some food for thought. Let me also make it abundantly clear that we were all created with free will and I am not trying to convince you to have faith in what you can't see. Instead I simply ask that you entertain the thought, toss around the concepts provided here and keep an open mind. When we open our minds to new ideas and ways of thinking, magical things begin to happen.

If you are unsure how you feel about whether to believe in something that cannot be seen, let me ask the following. Have you ever been afraid? Have you feared that you would fail or that something would go wrong?

Why would you believe in fear if it was not something that you could touch or see? Why would you believe in something that may not have even been real? You see, we often put faith in things that we cannot see, and you may not even realize how often we do this. Sometimes we give greater credit to things that keep us from achieving what we desire because we put greater faith in irrational thoughts driven by fear.

Fear is something that you feel but cannot see or touch and we put faith in it and believe in it. We allow it to control us. How can we possibly disregard faith in a spiritual realm? Is believing in fear really any different than spiritual faith?

What I would like to postulate is that you consider this contrast of belief or faith in that which doesn't seem to make sense and that what you cannot see to what you so easily seem to accept, fear and doubt. The greatest difference between the two, spiritual belief and faith from doubt and fear is that doubt and fear hold you back, wherein pure faith and belief move you forward.

The positive energy of faith and belief through the spiritual realm keeps things in motion, whereas fear and doubt stop energy in its tracks. I like to use the example of a lightning storm. When positive and negative ions collide, we get thunder and lightning. Positive energy won't be stopped, and we see a lightning bolt of energy burst from the sky as the negative energy tries to stop the positive motion. You and I were meant to move in positive energy and not be stopped in our tracks by fear. If you are going to choose to believe in one or the other, why not choose the one that is going to help you manifest your dreams?

The spiritual realm exists in parallel to our physical world. There are many dimensions to our universe that we cannot see. However, because our earth is what we can visually see, we assign that as a priority. Again, we are trained as a child that if we cannot see it, we must dismiss it. If we cannot see it, then it cannot exist or be real. So why is fear so natural? In our most basic instinct, we know there is more to life. We know there is someone or something at the helm, a source. This is why most have such faith that they can absolutely proclaim that there is a heaven. We just feel it. It's something that resonates and stirs within. It's a core belief that we hold strong and we just know. Yet here we are, dismissing that the universe cannot help us achieve our goals.

Take a close look at what you believe, is it fear that is keeping you from elevating your spiritualism? Is it fear that keeps you from believing in what you cannot see? Kind of hypocritical now that you realize that fear operates under the same framework of a belief.

Could it be that you cannot think past heaven's gates? Does heaven become your roadblock as if when you believe in it, you have committed to something? What I am saying here is that if you are to ever achieve your dreams, you must push forward and out of your mindset that solidifies everything in concrete.

Concrete thinking, black or white, will do nothing but keep you from achieving what you dream of. You must accept a belief that more than what you can see, and touch exists. If the thought of heaven holds you back because the picture in your mind forces you to say it's either this way or its not, then stop forcing yourself to put heaven in a box with four walls. Think of heaven with no limits, not as a structure. Stop trying to make things in your mind conform to the way you think they should be. The universe is much freer than that, and so are you.

Think of yourself as energy! You and everything around you are vibrating at a level that the eye cannot see. Even the words that you speak send out a vibration to the universe, and the universe responds. If you have ever seen a visual decibel meter as music is playing, you have witnessed the up and down motion as sound patterns are charted.

Many of us have heard that if you speak to your plants that they will grow faster and healthier. However, there is a twist. In 2014, the popular show Mythbusters© produced an episode that explored the possibility that plants respond to speech. The show hosts set up multiple greenhouses, four of which were equipped with stereos playing looped recordings wherein two were of negative speech, while two were of positive speech. The fifth greenhouse had classical music playing. The sixth had heavy death metal. Finally, a seventh greenhouse, set up as the control specimen, had no music. The team found that the plants in the four greenhouses with recordings grew faster than the control plants and that the plants in the greenhouses with music, grew even faster. The plants exposed to heavy metal grew the best out of all. Why do you think that is? Energy.

Words, regardless of positive or negative, have energy attached to them. If you have every listened to heavy metal, you'd find it's not the most positive, soothing music. It is very fast, rhythmic music, precisely why the plants grew the most! They responded to decisive, rhythmic energy.

How the plants responded to sound in the experiment is also how the universe responds to your goals, dreams, and deepest desires. If you simply write down your goals (which I do recommend) but you never look at them again, you will not reach any of your goals. To activate the spiritual realm, you must bring the energy of heavy metal to it. Be consistent, and be repetitive. Like the plants, your dreams require energy, and they desire pulsing, continually-driving energy to thrive.

Many think of the spiritual realm as this way-off, mystical realm that cannot be reached, but the fact is that it is right here, right now. There is nothing that you must do to 'get there', you are in it, it is around you, but the trick is to better understand how you can interact with it to manifest what you truly want.

Just like when you are learning to drive a car or play an instrument, at first you think, "I'm not sure if I can figure all this stuff out and remember what to do." Somehow we shift from uncertainty to auto-pilot. If you have ever driven home and thought, "Wow, I don't remember half of that drive," then you know what I mean. At some point what seemed unnatural and mentally taxing became second-nature.

I'm sure you have heard the phrase, "I can do that with my eyes closed." Or, "I could do that in my sleep." These phrases indicate that something becomes so known to us that we no longer need the use of our senses, touch, sight, smell, or hearing to do it. The spiritual realm can become that to you; where you can tap in on auto-pilot, without even thinking.

Courting Your Desires

Dreams exist because you think of them, but it is the energy that you put into them that breathes life into your dreams. So how do we increase our vibrational energy enough that our dreams move beyond a virtual concept to a physical manifestation of reality? Think of your dreams like a new love or a budding relationship.

What do you do? You court your new love. You spend time and energy learning everything you can about your new love. You eat, sleep, and dream about this person. They consume your mind. This is exactly how you increase your vibration, letting the universe know, this is what I want. This is what I desire to become reality.

There is a metaphysical connection between what we physically see and what we desire. Likely there is also the same quantum connection. Metaphysics is a branch of philosophy concerned with the nature of being, whereas quantum physics is concerned with how minute particles (quanta) interact. The connection between what cannot be seen is as real and concrete as what you see around you at this very moment.

The quantum realm is going on all around and through you. You are a part of a great interaction. Think of the blood coursing through your veins. The cells of your body are continually interacting, and you are a part of that and it is a part of you. You cannot separate yourself from your cells, nor can you separate yourself from the quanta.

If you want to change your physical shape, what do you do? You decide that you want to lose weight, gain muscle, and slim and tone. You begin to eat differently and begin an exercise program. Why? You do this because you need to influence change within the cells and the physical structure of your cells. But you cannot see your cells. You can see the outward manifestation of poor muscle tone or fat, but you cannot see the cellular level shift as you begin doing something different, yet, change is happening.

When you decided to make a change, your belief changed. You resolved that by increasing your activity level and decreasing your intake, that you could make change in your body. Why do we not believe that we can do this with anything else? The same metaphysical beliefs in the existence of a state that we have not experienced yet is tied to the same physiological and quantum level experience. What you believe connects to the energy of the things around you. You have the same power over everything you desire. It all begins with a thought and the following thoughts help pave the way. Thoughts are not the connecting piece between what is desired and what manifests; they are only a piece.

There is an amazing force within each of us. I am reminded by the famous line in Star Wars when the ominous Darth Vader stated, "Don't underestimate the Force." Further, Obi-Wan Kenobi introduced, young Jedi, Luke Skywalker to the force. "It's an energy field created by all living things. It surrounds us and penetrates us; it binds the galaxy together." Finally, Han Solo proclaimed, "That's not how the Force works!" Before you run out and binge-watch the entire Star Wars trilogy, let me help you understand this force.

The force within us has an unending and enduring composition. I Corinthians 13:7, states, "Love never gives up." Although it does not end, we can fail to recognize the power that it has over our reality. "The power of love, as the basis of a State, has never been tried" wrote Ralph Waldo Emerson. "A heart that reaches out with love can heal a soul and change a life" said Kiran Shaikh. Love is a powerful force. It is the central force and pulse of all existence.

Love is infinite. There is no beginning and end. There is nothing stronger nor more capable of the greatest joys and the greatest evils. How can this be so? Let's go back to the human body cell analogy to illustrate how this works.

If you cut your finger, the cells of the body go rushing toward the imperfect state, the injury, to render immediate healing. Within seconds the blood begins to clot to stop the bleeding and begin the healing process. This is because our natural state is one of a perfect, whole being. We are not meant to be partial or damaged, so repair begins automatically. If love equals your perfect state, then anything that opposes that state is hate, but these are not two separate things. Love and hate are connected, as hate is just the desire for the perfect state. It's like disappointment. What disappointment really is a state of desire for the opposite.

There is a natural order for positive, corrective energy in the universe, and that is love. Positive thinking is not a trick to the mind, it is its natural state, but many tend to forget this. We feel good when things go our way. When they don't, not so much so. When we are in love, we are on top of the world. When a lover wrongs us, anger and hurt set in. When we feel separated from our loving natural state, we can become jealous, envious, and lash out against those we love. We often do this to ourselves because we don't understand that we are the ones controlling our natural state.

Hate is not a derivative of love. It is the flip-side, as if there were a mirror of extremes. Hate is the direct opposite of love, as it is a yearning state of love. Hate is a separation of the love energy.

The manifestation of hate is a result of the opposing equal power, love, because it longs to be in a perfect state - love. So, am I saying that we hate and love at the same time? Yes. Because hate recognizes that it is absent of its natural state and needs to heal toward love. The darts of hate are defensiveness because of separation from love.

If love is a power so strong that people can physically manifest superhuman strength to save lives, hate has the same superhuman manifestation abilities to destroy lives. The point is that this power or force is so strong that miracles have been performed and whole groups of people have been destroyed. The latter is not the natural state of the universe. The natural state is the positive energy side of love.

When new in love you can't get enough of your lover. The energy is intoxicating. As love matures, the bonded energy takes deeper rooting. The foundational energy is so strong that opposing forces have no standing chance. Imagine if love were so strong in groups of people, hate could not flourish. It would be extinguished.

When we dream and desire, the binding agent is the force, our loving energy within. Uniting a loving energy, excitement, anticipation, longing, joy, and hope are all positive loving feelings that draw more positivity to them like a magnet.

Fear and doubt, connected to the absence of love feeling of hate, can reside below the surface and within our thoughts. I can't, I won't, I'm not sure, I don't know how… these are all manifestations of a cut to the finger. Will you allow the cells to rush to your aid? Will you choose to court what you desire? Putting in the forefront of your thoughts what you want?

It's okay. Long for your lover to return. This is your perfect state. Long for the new job. Long for that big house on the hill. Long for health. The key is to crush hate, doubt, fear, and the feeling that you don't deserve what you desire, by only exploring the side of life that you want- a loving, perfect state.

Please don't get hung up on the word perfect. When we get hung up on such things we put up roadblocks where they need not be. Understand that perfection is okay and is not necessarily a psychotic state of unreal conditional expectations. It is far different to long to meet a perfect mate that is "perfect" for you, considering what you deeply desire, than to be "perfect" in the eyes of other's expectations or desires. Perfection is a perceived state. Perfect is a state of natural balance.

Binding together your desires by connecting what you believe is the key to engaging and exciting the quanta. It is like a big ball of energy. The force is strong, and like Darth Vader said, "The force is strong with this one." This *one* is you.

Everything starts with a dream.

4 CULTIVATING YOUR DESIRES

Understanding how we connect in the big scheme of things is the first step in figuring this whole manifestation thing out. Cultivating your dreams requires not only spiritual work, but a lot of elbow grease. We are body, soul, and spirit, so we must look at each of those elements when making our dreams a reality.

I have met many people who have worked and toiled, putting in hard physical work trying to achieve their goals. On the flip side, I have met many others who thought that if they prayed all day, that somehow, the universe would open up to them and bless them. However, it's much more complicated than that. "The Force does not work that way!" Sorry, I just had to get in another Star Wars illustration. It is a balance of all three, and once we achieve balance, the universe will act like a giant vacuum and bring everything to your doorstep; faster than you can imagine.

So how do you start? First you must examine yourself and honestly find out what your strengths are, in physical body, soul, and spirit. Take me for example. I am someone who loves to work hard. If there is a task to do, I am the first one to take it on. I catch myself saying yes and then realizing that I'm in busy mode. I find myself taking on mindless, busy work, wherein what I am doing does not really seem to be getting me any closer to my dreams. I'm just really busy. This can throw us out of balance and out of the cultivation zone. To get back in balance, the first thing we need to start with is the most obvious aspect, and the one most often is put on the back burner, the soul.

Soul work can be the hardest principle to get, because we must really take a hard look at our inner core. It can be tough to really look at our true self, the self we often bury because of our life choices, or memories tied to painful experiences. Nonetheless, those experiences are often tied to our soul work.

Life isn't an easy path and it's not meant to be. There is learning to do and lessons to share. How can you learn without experience? How can you share if you haven't learned? Knowledge from reflection, self-awareness, honesty, and humility can often be the most valuable.

When we plant seeds, we do so expecting a harvest. Yet, if we do not care for our crops and provide everything they need, we will not be cultivating anything but crop-less soil. We must plant and nurture our desires, attending to the needs of our desires, with ongoing attention. It is this focus that is on purpose that yields the crop.

If a farmer just simply dropped a few seeds into the soil, never to tend to the seeds, chances are, the seeds would not yield anything. Sure, there are some plants that thrive in hostile environments, but it takes certain favorable conditions for even these to take root and grow. Conversely, if the farmer prepares the soil, plants the seeds, waters, and tends to the soil, the focus and intent of producing a crop yields a crop. We can't just plant and run. This is like just sitting around praying and believing for a bumper crop.

Effort does not mean busy, but making an effort toward cultivating your dreams is necessary to manifest what you want. Clearing the weeds of disbelief, fears, and confusion is necessary. We cannot reap a harvest if our crop is being choked out at the roots. This happens more than you realize.

It's Just Below the Surface

Just below the surface of the seedling much can happen. Too much water and the plant suffocates. It drowns. Too little water and it withers and dies. Worms and grubs may eat into the little sprout of hope that just wants to break through to the surface into the warm sun that it feels calling above. Our dreams are just like this.

When we tend to the garden of our dreams we are keeping tabs on the condition of what is going on just below the surface. Our beliefs, accumulated through happy and painful life lessons live here- just below the surface.

Looking below the surface for anything that could damage our crops requires that we become reflective, self-aware, honest, humble, and willing to accept what we may find. This can be quite painful at times, but cultivating your desires will require that you understand your soil condition. Without self-awareness, you may feel like you are continually working on your garden, yet yielding no fruit.

What is self-awareness? This is not a question to be taken lightly. What is it to truly be self-aware? If a friend tells you about an event that happened to them, and in listening, you are applying what you know about your friend, strengths and flaws, your perspective will differ from your friend's perspective. This is because you are able to see what they cannot. When they ask you, "Was I wrong to do that?" This is their higher level of knowledge posing this question to them. Yet, instead, they are asking for your opinion.

When we begin to ask ourselves such questions. Did I handle that situation correctly? Should I have…? How do I feel about that? We begin to tap into our deeper truth, our higher knowledge. This can only be accessed through reflection. We must look inside, like looking into a pool of water. What do you see? Do you see something from a different perspective?

Perhaps the person that I offended thought this….I can see how when I said this….and that they thought that. Understanding how to evaluate what we do, how we think, why we think it, and how we react is imperative to growth and cultivation. When we harbor thinking that can hold us back, and don't know that we are holding onto this, we can't manifest what we want.

The beauty of reflection and self-awareness is that we can quickly see when something is happening beneath the surface that we don't want. We must be very much in tune to pick up on this and then willing to do whatever needs to be done to move forward.

Peeling back the layers like an onion or tilling the soil, these are actions. To peel back a layer of belief or to yank out a weed that is stealing nutrients from your desire means that you must be willing to take action. Pain and disappointment can be crippling. We often don't realize the residual effect is has. It isn't until we realize that the barrier coming between what we want and us is there that we can do something about it. As we become increasingly honest with ourselves about how something made us feel, we then begin to see where residue has manifest.

Hopes and Dreams

I recently took my grandkids to see the film Beauty and the Beast. I did not realize the profound effect the movie would have on me as I remembered how I enjoyed watching the Disney animated version wish my kids when they were young. I simply recalled a cute Disney movie.

It turned out to be a poignant moment of self-discovery, of disappointment, and broken hopes and dreams. Something that I teach my clients however, is that in every disappointment is a discovery of what they truly desire. So, for me, not only was it a moment of discovery of something still lingering under the surface, but also a moment to tap into what I really want.

I'm sure most of you know the tale of Beauty and the Beast. The Beast was once a prince, who had become so cruel by losing sight of what love, mercy, and beauty truly are that a sorcerous cast a spell on the prince, turning him into a beast and turning his caretakers into alternative forms.

The spell could only be broken when the Beast could truly love another and be loved in return. Desperate to get their lives' back, the care takers put hope into the Beast and his prisoner, Belle, making them fall in love and breaking the spell.

I viewed this movie from a new perspective. You see, three years ago, I survived escaping a domestic violence marriage. Watching the Beast change, accepting responsibility for his bad behavior, humbling himself to the shallow nature of his past, and learning from this was something that I desired of my ex-husband. Yet instead, he remained the Beast.

The movie moved me to tears, as something below the surface moved. Immediately I realized what it was, I yanked that weed, as if it were crabgrass and I wanted to get every last bit of the root so that it would not sprout again! This awakening may not have happened if I weren't at a high level of self-awareness. These are the types of feelings that can live beneath the surface, choking out what it is you desire.

If you had a business that you lost or a deal that fell through, the next time you are in a similar situation you may have something under the surface in the shape of a fear or disappointment hanging out, ready to choke out what you are trying to manifest.

The most important part of the cultivation process is self-reflection, checking the soil, feeling if there is something there that shouldn't be- just below the surface.

Our hopes and dreams can be derailed by our past or even the past of others. We accept beliefs based on what someone else experienced or has or hasn't been done before as use these excuses not to yield fruit. In reality, we poisoned our own soil. We allowed toxicity to thwart the growth of our dreams. Yes, this is a choice. Cultivation is on purpose. Believing in, going for, and getting what you desire is on purpose. This means that you need to dig around frequently for weeds in your garden.

The Self-Aware Gardener

Cultivating means that you prepare, sow, and reap your harvest. It means that you are fully aware of everything that goes into your crop. I personally like meditation, but there are many excellent techniques to help you become more self-aware not only of items below the surface but also in achieving clarity in what it is that you want.

One technique for beginners is to shift from a lack perspective to a positive desire perspective. Although I call this a technique for beginners, this technique is just one of the most simple to apply to building your self-awareness. I, in no way am implying that this technique will only provide beginner results, because as you grow, so too can this technique.

Think about something that you don't like. Let's take for example, stubbing your toe. It hurts! You might jump around and maybe grab your toe and rub it. But what are you really doing? You are giving attention to the hurt toe. Like a three-year old screaming and kicking on the floor at Walmart because he didn't get a toy, your toe is calling out the same way. Like my puppy going through training, start yelling, "Leave it!"

You lost a sale. The customer, for whatever reason decided not to buy the product from you, even though you have put many hours into providing him information. It's disappointing and everything in you is screaming, that sucks! Leave it!

Whether physical pain, psychological pain, heart-ache, or disappointment, there is a direct opposite: no pain, no heart-ache, and no disappointment. This is where you get to practice the shift. For every negative feeling, I want you to think about the opposite. No, this isn't a lesson in merely positive thinking. This is a lesson in becoming self-aware of the emotions or the physical pain, and what you would rather have.

I stub my toe. Ouch! Oh my gosh, that hurts. I want to be pain free. I want the pain to subside quickly. This is your desire. You realize that you DO NOT want pain. I'm going to be more careful next time. Self-awareness at its most basic form.

I lost a sale. I'm disappointed. I put so much time into that sale. Perhaps the person was not truly ready to buy, but is there something that I may have been able to say or do to influence even a luke-warm buyer? I would have really liked to have sold him that product. I'm going to do some research on turning cold looky-loos into red hot customers. Shifting your focus away from the hurt and disappointment and to what you want will help you in achieving what you want.

Now, what if that non-sale made you feel like less of a salesperson? What if this was just one of a series of lost sales. Not only are you feeling like a complete loser, now you are worried that your lack of sales performance could cost you your job. In this situation you may have lots of garbage in your soil. You can bury it and say that it doesn't bother you, but if it does, you better deal with it or no crop for you!

Honesty and humility can be tough. When we are having a tough time with something, it pays to be honest with what the situation is. I'm single. I don't care for not having a partner. I desire love. I want to have a long-term, committed relationship, that is emotionally healthy, full of passion, romance, friendship, trust, and respect. I respect myself too much to condone the bad behavior of others. I will have healthy, friendly relationships, while being happy with me, yet working to continually be a better me, until my dream manifests.

We don't have to go through a whole Negative Nancy list about what is wrong with ourselves. In fact, honesty and humility does not mean that we need to be demeaning of ourselves. If you have some jerk-like attributes, be big enough to own up, but don't hold yourself down. Take note, pick yourself up and present yourself in front of your mirror with humility to become better. Honesty and humility simply means that we open up to what we truly desire, address any areas that we may want to improve, and make an action plan to do so.

It is very helpful to develop a list of what you like, appreciate, and care for as you are increasing your self-awareness. Focus on these feelings quite often as these are what will provide energy to your desires. If you want love, focus on the aspects of love that excite everything in you. Focus on the aspects that give you that amazing feeling.

Think of this as how you felt as a kid with a present that you couldn't wait to open at Christmas. It was so exciting. You just wanted to know what was inside. It made you feel happy, excited, and like you had a big ball of energy tossing around just bursting to get out! This is how anticipating what you desire with a joyful heart should be like.

Engaging and connecting to the powerful force of appreciation and joy is extremely helpful during your self-awareness shifts. Not only will your level of joy, contentment, and appreciation increase for so much more around you, but you will also begin shifting much easier to a much more productive state of mind. You will be ready to cultivate your dreams-yielding a bounty of harvest.

Protecting Your Dreams from Varmints

You prepare the soil, plant the seeds, nurture the seeds with nutrients, water, warmth, sunlight, and you pull the weeds. It seems like your garden is perfect and you should reap a bountiful harvest of dreams. What could possibly go wrong? Pests and varmints that do not care about your garden. They are just hungry and destructive, and they will attempt to ravage your garden.

It would be so great if I could tell you to dream big and everyone around you would believe in your dreams, but that's not usually the reality. Why is it that other people want to be such buzz-kills? Some people in our lives truly believe that they are *helping* by *protecting* you from *disappoint.* Sure, doesn't feel much like *helping* when it happens, it feels defeating.

There are yet others that don't even disguise their sabotaging of your dreams, they just swoop right in and deliver a crushing blow. Napalm! Wiped that crop right out!

Protecting your dear little seedlings can be a daunting task, like protecting your rose garden from deer or aphids and your lawn from pocket gophers. Keeping those that would like to chomp away at your seedlings, whether intentionally or to *help you out*, is a never-ending task. You must remain vigilant in protecting your *dreamlings.*

Even after your little *dreamlings* blossom and fruit and you reap a harvest of manifested dreams, your garden is not without risk. Dream manifestation is not seasonal, it is an ongoing rotation of crops. You will need to protect your soil with cover crops during the winter so that you can amend your soil with rich nutrients to produce your next bounty.

Have you ever accomplished or achieved something that you were incredibly proud of, only to have someone make a comment that brought you down? Negative comments, concerns, and criticisms can eat away at you. This can make you wonder if you are worthy of what you manifest. It can make you feel greedy and selfish. Other's words can wipe out every bit of effort that you put into manifesting your dream as you begin questioning your validity. Do you really deserve what you desire?

It's not necessarily that people don't want you to succeed, although there truly are some people who don't want to see you get something that they don't have, but many people are so inhibited by barriers to their thinking that they speak fear in defense. They don't want you to fail, but if you try, then you might fail, so they speak fear.

What you believe, you begin to create. What you can see, you put into action. The quantum world does not know the difference between real pictures in your head of what you have experience and pictures in your head that you are imagining. So, when a negative comment is hurled your way that makes you question whether you deserve what you have or what you desire, and yes, what you have already manifest, it destroys and weakens your ability to generate and maintain your dreams. My suggestion? Keep those varmints out of your garden!

Deer fences exist and are quite tall for a reason, because Bambi can jump, HIGH! We had such a pocket gopher problem in my yard that we excavated all the dirt several inches, laid down chicken wire, constructing a huge hamster cage, laid the dirt back down, and then the grass on top. Where I wanted to put in plants, I dug the hole, constructed a wire cage to fit the hole, and planted the plant. I was sick of my yard being destroyed! Why would we not be just as serious about keeping other people's thinking out of our heads?

Other people's fear does not belong to you. Remember, fear will separate you from your desires. What you sow is what you will reap. If you take in fearful thinking, your results will reflect fearful thinking. Your results will be lacking substance and reality.

What is reality? Let's break this down so that you understand how important constructing barriers from fearful thinking is. Reality is a belief that has manifest into something tangible. When we dream, we have a desire, and when we believe that we can achieve what we desire, we have set into motion that action. What happens then when we fear? Or when someone introduces us to fear, where no fear existed before? If we accept it, it becomes a belief. We can't accept a belief in a desire and at the same time accept fear that we can't achieve the desire. The thoughts are negated, and the dream is defeated.

If I achieve and manifest what I have desired, yet then accept fear, I will lose what I have manifes.t Guess what? I have just nullified my dream and it will begin to erode. Why? Because I accepted an opposing belief which will spring into action.

The garden of your dreams and desires is worth protecting. Manifesting your dreams requires vigilance. This is what you want. Protect it when the seed has just been planted and long after the harvest has been reaped. Keep the dream alive by continuing to believe, be joyful, and share your harvests. You'll be amazed out how quickly those doubters will become believers as you share with them your secret.

Dreams are often most profound when they seem the most crazy.

5 PIPE DREAM OR REALITY? WHAT'S THE DIFFERENCE?

What you desire cannot be judged as realistic or not, regardless of the size of the dream. People often refer to a dream that seems non-sensical or too big to understand as a pipe dream. Just because it has not been done does not mean that it can't or won't. Can we really dream too big?

The history of the pipe dream can be traced to the strange, lucid, and hallucinogenic dreaming experienced by smokers of opium pipes. These dreams were thought to be impractical or impossible. What is illustrated by the pipe dream or any other dream, for that matter, that does not meet other's criteria as achievable or sensible, is that judgement can make the difference between what is a pipe dream or reality.

Where would we be had the visions of Steve Jobs, Albert Einstein, or the Wright Brothers, been judged and then abandoned? There will always be critics, but the difference between the reality you desire coming to fruition or being abandoned and disintegrating from your reality is the introduction of chaos to your now.

The Nexus to Manifest

Eckhart Tolle, in his book, *The Power of Now*, expressed the importance of living in the present moment and avoiding thoughts of the past and the future. Wallace D. Wattles, author of the 1903 book, *The Science of Getting Rich*, introduced *new thought* principles on how visualizing what you want can lead to manifestation of these thoughts. The principles were re-introduced by author Rhonda Byrne in her 2006 hit film *The Secret.* What seems to have been missed by many, as they have tried to explain these principles, is an interpretation and understanding of the nexus between our desires and our reality.

In his book, *Secrets of the Millionaire Mind*, T. Harv Eker provides the clearest definition of the nexus of desire and reality by postulating that the inside becomes the outside. There is much more to the concept of *what we think, we become*, than meets the eye. It is not simply thinking and desiring, it is the power of the nexus, and the power of the present state that drives the future.

The quanta are set into motion in the present. Your dream, no matter the size, is set into motion to become what you see at the nexus of past, present, and future. In this place is joy. At the nexus is where change happens. The nexus is the key to our desired state.

We are all one choice from our dreams and from our greatest challenges. Our free will, freedom of thought, and freedom of choice are all determined at the nexus of now and the future. What we think in the now, more importantly how we think, sets into motion our future. Your desired state is actualized now.

I believe why manifestation has been so misinterpreted and oversimplified into *see it and it will be*, is because the power of the nexus has not been fully articulated as the central component of the process in a manner that can be readily understood. After all, if everyone really *got it*, then everyone would certainly be in a continual state of manifestation.

The nexus is the missing link in common manifestation teaching. The power of now is because now is at the nexus. What you desire only exists when you create it. The only time and place to create is now. The biggest problem is that our own thinking gets in our way.

Every decision that we make is at the nexus. For most of us, we go about making decisions with little to no thought of how we are thinking. We just do it. We just think and act.

The concept of random acts of kindness is nothing new, but what we don't think of when we randomly make a choice to be kind, is the power of the choice in the now, and what that sets into motion for the future. More importantly, do we even put any thought into what we are setting into motion?
Random acts of kindness are thoughts that set into motion a *pay it forward effect.* A choice of kindness

today sets forth into motion a boomerang effect of kindness toward us in the future. When we see beyond ourselves and choose to be kind, not for what we receive, but just for the sake of it, we are not randomly selecting to be kind, but instead we are setting ourselves up to randomly receive a kind act. Why not receive what we want on purpose and with intent? This can only be set into motion at the nexus.

Our choice to be kind is created from joy in the now and therefore we set into motion the creation of kindness. Kindness exists when you choose to create it. It doesn't end because you quit thinking about being kind, it transcends time and multiplies and compounds.

Our dreams and desires are the same as choosing to create kindness. The birthplace of our desires and dreams is in our thoughts, at the nexus. The nexus is only reachable from the present. It is for this reason that other teachers on manifestation state that it is necessary to speak of our desires as if they already exist.

It's not a matter of just stating your desire as if it exists, you must realize the present state. Becoming mentally aware of the present is the key to access the nexus in the future. I could go on and on about meditation for so many reasons, but the main one is to get you to the point where you can realize your presence at the nexus.

Teachers of manifestation instruct their followers to state your intention and what you want while visualizing its existence as if you already have received or achieved the desire. This is correct, but you must first enter the nexus. You must also interrupt any thinking that appears in this place that does not serve you. Let me lead you through an activity to practice this.

If you are not already, go to a place that is free of distractions. My favorite time to do this is right when I wake up. I like to lay in bed to do this activity as it is a wonderful way to start the day. Wherever you do this, just make sure you are free of distractions. The more you practice, you will be able to access from wherever you are.

Once you are in a distraction-free place, close your eyes and take a few deep breaths. In this place, focus your thoughts on where you are. Feel how you feel, right now. Is the room warm, cool, or just perfect? What are the sensations of your experience right now?

As you feel the sensations of your current *now* experience, begin to introduce thoughts of appreciation. Try starting out with something like this: "I appreciate waking to a new day, a new beginning, and my bright new future. I appreciate being provided another day to achieve."

An appreciative state is a place of joy. Appreciation is connected to love, the driving energy of the universe. As we offer up appreciative praise for what we have, even if all we can seem to muster up at first is to be appreciative for another day, our vibration and energy increase. Love and joy are ignited when we are appreciative.

Let's think about that. If someone thanks you for offering assistance or you are given an award of appreciation, it feels good. Why is that? Appreciation is an expression of love. The residual effect is joy and happiness. When we open up our mind to our *now* by offering appreciation, we increase the vibrational energy of the quanta.

Primed and ready to go, once we have increased our vibration into the universe, within our now, the focus of our thoughts is in the present state for our desires. An example would be to state, "I love that I am focused on optimizing my health and healthy body weight." Or, "I am excited to be the candidate selected for the position. I know I am the perfect person for the job."

The way you state what you desire is more important than what you actually desire. Believable statements are the most important. If I were to say something like, "I am the smartest person for the job," yet I don't believe it, I have negated my *now* statement.

It is important to learn to phrase your statements so that the little voice of doubt inside your head (ego) doesn't point out flaws in your statements. This is where the interruption of negative thinking happens. You must believe your *now* statements. Adding words that describe your feelings are also powerful.

Our mind is designed to connect elements. Every thought has an associated feeling and every feeling is born from a thought. Connecting our phrased thoughts to how having that thought would makes you feel, increases the vibration of your desire.

"I am excited....I am joyful.... I am happy...." Each of these statements preceding the thought, help to turn up the power as you launch creation into the quantum field. Our thoughts are powerful, especially when we learn the power of our present state.

In our present state we cannot dream too big. In our present state there is no room for judgment because once judging thoughts enter, you have exited the now. Ego and judgment cannot exist in the present state.

Ego will always direct you to the past or to the future. A simple thought like, "but you don't know how," is an ego-driven judgment that is trying to drag you backwards. Judgment that you don't know means that in the past you haven't learned, so therefore your future cannot be, because you are not good enough.

Do you see how tricky the ego is? It is such a crafty trickster that we go about our day being conned on a regular basis. Our dreams and desires are annihilated by judgment without our even being aware. Pipe dream? Says who?

The pipeline to our dreams is at the nexus. There is no dream too big or too small, there are only dreams, realities waiting to be created. It's your job to be present and find your now so that your dreams can be created.

Creating Your Reality

What is reality? Is it what you see or is it what you believe? Can reality remain unseen but exist? Or does reality only exist if there is acknowledgement and acceptance?

Most dreams are crushed because of dream-crushing thoughts. When we doubt that we can achieve or lack faith in our abilities, we disable our dreams by disengaging creation at the nexus. Doubt can be automatic as it is built into the body's defense mechanisms to keep us free from hurt.

I'd like to clarify the difference between untrue thoughts and dream-crushing thoughts. Have you ever got caught up in "what-if" thoughts that put your mind into a wild tailspin? These thoughts can get you so caught up in thinking that the "what-if" scenario is certain. These "what-if" thoughts, if based in negativity and fear, will drag you backwards. They will pull you into the past, even though you believe that you are thinking of the future. Let me be clear, fear-based thoughts are untrue. I like to call these insane thoughts

A sane thought would be one based on the reality of your circumstances, something that you are working towards achieving, not something that you fear might happen. Believing more in what bad could happen, rather than what you want, is not rational. Why would you focus and believe in something that you do not want to happen more than what you do want? Pretty insane, right?!

The way fear-based thinking, especially around "what-if" and other speculative scenarios, drags you into the past is by the thoughts using shame, regrets of past failures, disappointments, and mis-steps against you. This thinking points out to your ego your weaknesses, and amplifies them. This type of fearful thinking is not based on actual reality, instead your mind begins to create a new reality of what you don't want. Learning to control your thought patterns and identify when these thoughts are not serving you will help you to create the reality that you want instead of the reality that you do not.

Dream-crushing thoughts are untrue thoughts that you create as a self-protection mechanism. If you never take a chance at failing, you will never experience disappointment. You will also never gain the most valuable experience, the experience of what did not work. Fearing failure is fearing success because we must first fail to succeed.

Believing that you can't succeed or that opposition to what you want will happen, will negate any positive thoughts of success. Freezing this thinking is imperative to get you to where you want to be – in a successful mindset – a manifestation mindset. This is not simply a matter of positive thinking. Creating the reality that you desire is a matter of intentional thought and intentionally monitoring any thoughts that are counterproductive.

Our thoughts can run rampant in our brains like pre-school children running around unsupervised. There is no telling what harm can happen when we aren't paying attention. Our thoughts, unsupervised, will tend to gravitate toward the ruts and previous neuro-pathways. To get out of the rut we must guide our thinking to the path that we want our thinking to travel so that we create the reality that we desire.

Taking control of our thinking requires that you accept a few concepts: 1) you are worthy, and 2) sometimes things that seem too good to be true actually can happen – we just need to accept that we are worthy of these great things. Worthiness is often, what I like to liken to, a rubber band in the brain. We are going about our lives, happy, and then something snaps, and we go right back to an "I knew it was too good to be true mindset." Why do we do this to ourselves? Why are we so hard on ourselves? Simply put, we have a rubber band in our mind stuck to a belief that we aren't good enough.

Facebook CEO, Sheryl Sandberg speaks in her book, *Lean In*, how many women hold a belief that they aren't worthy to hold the same jobs as men. This belief is formed from the past where traditionally, men ran companies, and women were school teachers, mothers, and nurses. Many women still buy-in to beliefs of inadequacy when competing for a job against a strong male figure. It's all in the mind, and it's all attributed to a belief of unworthiness.

A study was done a few years back that the evaluated perspectives of managers and executives. There was an overwhelming commonality among even the most confident of professionals. The majority of the executive felt like they would be found to be frauds. This thinking was not based on reality, but rather, deep-seated beliefs of not being good enough. Because these leaders did what they did, with relative ease, the "it's too good to be true" thinking popped up, attached to a rubber band of unworthiness.

Are the majority of executives and managers incompetent? I would venture to say, no. Feeling like you are going to be "found out" is a common feeling, and is not based on reality. It is common to compare ourselves to others and to develop feelings of inadequacy based on comparison. Again, most of the time, these are irrational thoughts. What's important to note is that feelings of inadequacy are usually rooted in fear-based thinking – fear of failure, fear of not being good enough, undermining our effectiveness and our ability to tap into our true desires.

Creating the reality that we desire means that we need to deconstruct destructive thinking lodged in fear and doubt. Accepting that you were created worthy and remain worthy is step one. Step two is to accept that things that exceed our wildest dreams do exist. Sometimes things that seem too good to be true actually can happen – and you can create this reality.

Reality does not need to be based on what already is, reality is what we create, and creation begins now. Reality is what you accept and believe to be true. For this reason, dream-crushing thoughts, doubts and fear, drive away belief and invite in disbelief. If you want to manifest what you desire, you must choose thoughts that you believe. One of the most effective ways to reinforce what you desire to become your reality is to sandwich your current reality with your desired reality.

Sandwiching is an amazing manifestation technique and it can work wonders for helping shift your feelings about your circumstances, clearing doubt and dream-crushing thoughts, and helping shift your thinking to a more productive reality creating realm. Let me explain how this works. As stated previously, manifestation is not simply a matter of thinking a thought and it is coming into existence, it is a matter of creating beliefs and then turning those beliefs into reality.

Sandwiching takes a desire that you feel strongly about that already exists and enveloping your desires around that thought. The next layer is to create a desiring thought that does not currently exist in your reality. The next step is to sandwich in the thought that you desire to become reality in another desire that already exists. I will give you an example of what this looks like.

First, I will state something that I have in a manner that is a desiring thought. "I would love to have an amazing career as a life coach." I then follow that thought with a feeling that supports why I desire the what I desire. "Being a coach would feel great as I am able to help people reach for their dreams and achieve their goals."

Since I already have an amazing career as a life coach, this thought, belief, is easy for my subconscious mind to accept. There is no doubt, rather, I feel a sense of completeness and accomplishment because I have what I desire. I created that reality.

Next, I will state something that I am yet to accomplish. "I want to make $50 million per year annual income." I can then follow this statement with how this would make me feel. "It would be great to have an annual income of $50 million per year from my coaching business and my books because the more I make, the more I can do for others, and the financial freedom will allow me to do more for my family."

As I state what I want and connect that to a desire in the present, I am beginning the creation process. By immediately following with something that I have, I sandwich in what is and what I desire to be. In essence, by sandwiching, the mind sees both equally. If you want to manifest, begin practicing desiring thought sandwiches with what you already have, but had previously dreamed of having, and what you desire to have.

Sandwiching your desires helps to break the rubber band of unworthiness as it conditions your mind to see that you are a creator. Once you believe in your power to create, you will begin to create your reality on purpose. Just think of a time when you really wanted something badly. What did you do? You focused on that thing and took actions to make what you wanted to happen. You already know that you are able to create your own reality. Unfortunately, we become conditioned over time to believe that what we end up with is luck, happenstance, or just the way things panned out.

Nothing just happens. We created everything we see. We also can destroy our dreams by doubting that we are worthy or that we can. Go ahead and believe that sometimes things that seem too good to be true can happen – and they happen when you make them happen by desiring, believing, and being relentless in your pursuit of making your dreams your reality.

Live beautifully and dream passionately.

6 MAKING YOUR MARK-
A GREAT BIG WORLD

None of us were born to be small in this world. We weren't created to simply take up space on this planet, or in creation for that matter. We have a destiny to create, to manifest and leave our mark through our creation. We were created in the image of God, the creator. That means that we are, in fact, creators.

It's true that in the vastness of the universe, and the entire quantum existence that we are a mere speck, but we are anything but insignificant. Our creator is the Great I Am! We are creators of our world in every thought that we prescribe and every meaning that we assign. So why would we stop there?

Who we are and what we create becomes a part of the bigger picture. As born creators, we are created perfect, with no fear, and in the image of God. We have a deep knowing that we have a purpose to contribute to this great big world. Our inner self is that beautiful child in all of us, so close to its real self when we are young, but somewhere in between our creation and the development of belief systems we become lost.

Feeling lost or without purpose is extremely common. If you want proof of this, just do a Google search on finding your purpose. You will come up with somewhere in excess of 388,000,000 results! That's because so many people are searching for something that they just can't put their finger on. They can't quite figure out what it is that they are supposed to be doing here.

So how exactly do we become so lost if we know that we have a purpose when we are created? Doesn't it seem like we should retain this knowledge? Who's to say that the knowledge is lost?

How is it as a child we wanted to conquer the day, and then as adults we wanted to conquer the world with our ambition, and then we get to the point of just wanting to be left alone? How do we become so lost and complacent?

When was the last time that you let yourself play like a child? A time when you didn't have a care in the world about who was watching you, how you looked, or what other people were thinking. A time when you let your imagination run wild and you actively participated in your imaginary world – you played there. When was the last time you watched a butterfly in wonderment as you could feel the beautiful energy flowing from its fluttering wings?

As we experience all of the amazing things this world has to offer in way of feelings and sensations, and absorb knowledge from our physical and emotional interactions with our world, we become distracted. We become derailed from our purpose. We become fearful and doubtful of pursuing, creating, and dreaming, when that is what we were intended to do! It's no wonder we have this aching longing. It's like some hidden treasure that we feel that we are searching to uncover, but it's there. It's inside of you – your inner knowledge never left. You are just creating distance, like a chasm between you and what you know.

The world can tend to dish out sadness and hardship and if we allow our thinking to be run by our circumstances, we are robbed of our joy and the gap between us and our calling widens.. If you let yourself be run by circumstances, your thoughts will run amuck like a two-year old running through the house unsupervised. Inevitably, something bad is going to happen in this situation, but we have the power to reign this back in. You can control your destiny and take back your power.

This starts by stopping the insanity. For one, stop running in a million directions, trying to be something to everyone, yet feeling unfulfilled. When you do this, you are derailed from your divine purpose. When we allow what everyone else wants to become a priority, or when everything hits the fan and we let our reactive mode become our driving force, we lose our focus on manifesting what it is that we want and that which we were intended to create.

Dream manifestation is your absolute right and destiny. Creation is the natural order of our existence and when we aren't manifesting, something is out of order. Making your mark in this world is achieved through clarity of purpose and desire.

Creating a clear vision of how you will leave your impression on this world is much simpler than you would think, but in this hurry up and get things done now society, we simply rush past opportunities to gain clarity and manifest.

Awareness and consciousness of what is, is the key to clarity. You'd be shocked by just how stopping and sitting still, and quieting the mind, can help tease out the thoughts running through your head in the background. These thoughts are the key to achieving clarity and moving you in your purpose.

So much of our self-worth and identity is tied up in what we do for others and how they perceive us. Ask yourself this question: What is it that you would give up, and why? Tackling each of these thoughts is the only way you can deal with your attachment to an issue or role that was never meant for you.

If you look at the great leaders and organizations of the world, there is one constant theme to their success. They started with the most basic of questions, and that is "Why." For so long we instinctively know what we do, and we know how we do it, but it's knowing why we do it that helps us find our own rhythm of our life.

When you can find the why of a cause, a belief, a purpose, you begin to communicate differently. Your body and every cell within it begin to take hold. You begin by communicating inside from your core and transcending it outward. Those who inspire are tapping into that, and it will change how you move through the world forever.

Engaging your body, mind, and spirit, bringing your full authentic self forward, is the only way to tolerate personal growth. Take a look at people making a difference that inspire you. Make a list, write down the characteristics of each of these people. What are the common core themes that arise? The one that is constant on my list is they are authentic. They spend most of their lives about kindness, caring and contributing something to make the world a better place. Worrying about who gets credit means your ego is not in check. The one who operates from integrity, empathy, and truthfulness, in service to others, will leave a large impression on the world.

Beliefs that Hold You Back

There are so many damaging beliefs that get stored in our subconscious. These come from experiences and interactions with others throughout our life time. To make our mark and to manifest what we want, instead of what we don't want, we must identify and address any damaging beliefs that we have within.

Deconstructing negative thoughts and beliefs that have become stored within our neuro processors begins with a trip within. When you think of why you believe you can't (can't what?) or you think of reasons and excuses for why you stopped yourself from pursuing a dream in the past, there are deeply embedded damaging beliefs to extract.

We extract damaging beliefs by interrupting their communication. Creating new thought patterns and pathways, deconstructing what we don't want, and building in what we do is done by abruptly replacing the picture, sentence, or memory with what we want. This is the element of manifestation that is critical, and the one that is never mentioned in other teachings.

As doubt and fear creep into your thinking as you are meditating in an affirmation state, immediately recognize that this old belief pattern must be interrupted. Just as if someone stepped in front of you when you are on your way to an important meeting, immediately recognize this is in my way and this is what I am doing instead. In the example of someone getting in your way, you would quickly take a step to the left or right and go around. There would be no hesitancy or question, you would just do it.

When we feel fear and doubt, this is the body's warning system to alert you that something inside you is trying to hold you back from your desire. Imagine if every time you desired to do something, a big, blue, hairy monster jumped in front of you. You would quickly recognize that a big, blue, hairy monster was there, right? Well, with practice and awareness, recognizing our unconscious negative beliefs can become just as obvious, but we must be willing to take action and interrupt that monster as soon as it appears.

Stop the beast in its tracks. It's holding you back from manifesting what you want. There is simply no way to state, "I desire …." and to hold onto negative beliefs that you cannot achieve or deserve what it is that you desire. Negative beliefs serve as a wrecking ball to your manifestation. Stop it mid-swing. Interrupt and reposition your thoughts.

Committing to Your Dreams

The surest way to stop the manifestation of your dreams is not going the distance.

"Constant repetition carries conviction" – Robert Collier.

Committing to your dreams to allow your manifestation to take place means that you are willing to go the distance and hold that belief no matter how long it takes.

Colonel Sanders, of KFC fame, submitted his famous, "secret recipe" to 1,009 restaurants before he got a *bite*. Walt Disney was fired from his first job because "he lacked imagination and had no good ideas." Vincent Van Gogh only sold one of his, more than 800 paintings, to a close friend.

Each of these people manifested what they believed in because not only did they believe and create in their *now*, what it was they wanted, but they interrupted any doubt and believed in their dreams no matter how long it took. Failure was not option. Manifestation was certain, and it was certain because they were certain and relentless in their persistent belief in their dreams.

Interrupting thoughts that impede manifestation and replacing these thoughts with unrelenting belief helps to reprogram our neuro pathways. This helps you to create new thought patterns that better serve your dreams. Again, this takes recognizing the big, blue, hairy monster when it appears. This might look like, "It's been six years. Maybe it's not meant to be."

Just remember, most break throughs happen one step beyond your breaking point. That's why it's called a break through. You pushed past the pain and the point that you didn't think that it was possible. The point is we must keep the faith. Keep believing even when what we see contradicts what it is we want.

Courage and Faith to Manifest

Believing in something so strongly, especially when every indication contradicts what you desire, takes courage. Finding the courage and strength to believe despite what others might say takes faith in your own beliefs. Again, you may have to identify monsters when they pop up.

Your dreams are worth being courageous for. Imagine yourself as a mighty warrior, dressed in armor and valiantly guarding your dreams. Shield and sword raised, you defend your beliefs when an opposing force (your damaging unconscious beliefs), appear.

Your faith in your belief runs strong and deep. You become unwavering in what it is that you want and your belief that it will manifest. As you create your imagery and see yourself in your dream, the quanta take form. Your dream exists – it is. The nexus has been engaged to create. It's now up to you to hold the faith and be courageous to continue believing until the axis of your dream and your reality converge into your present state.

Hold fast to the imagery of your dream. Feel it, engage your senses. Ruminate in it. Regularly visualizing yourself in your dream, as if your dream is your current reality, will help move your closer to the axis of manifestation. Do not let go of this. Your dream exists because you have the courage and faith to continue believing and to continue dwelling in your dream while awake.

Regularly practicing *dreaming while awake* visualization, will help you to keep the faith and keep your manifestation energy vibration in a high state of creation. To illustrate this, think of a football game, if the players were walking around the field in slow motion, the energy, not only on the field, but in the entire stadium would be low. It wouldn't exactly be an exciting game to watch, and more importantly, things would be moving so slowly that it would be impossible for anyone to advance, take possession, and score. Imagine being in the stands watching. There would be no anticipation, no excitement, and really no point in being there. No energy = no results.

Conversely, if the players are running the ball and tackling each other, the energy of both the players and the fans is high. The players are excited. The fans are excited. You can feel the energy of anticipation and excitement in the air. The energy is contagious and connected.

If you can, with excited anticipation, visualize your dream regularly, you can maintain a high state of creative energy and manifestation – no matter how long the process takes. Your energy is not only contagious within you and the quantum realm, but to others around you. Your relentless energy and belief in your dream will cause others to believe. This is how the unseen becomes the seen.

"When you see it in your head, you will see it in front of your eyes."

You are Limitless

The beauty of manifestation is that when you fully understand the law of creation and attraction, you will believe in your limitlessness. When you realize that you are limitless, your mark on this world takes on a whole new meaning. You fully understand how everything is connected through energy and how your passion drives it. The perpetual cycle of energy then takes passion to creation and creation to manifestation which reinforces and enhances passion so on and so on in an endless cycle.

We are limitless in what we can dream and what we can create. The only thing stopping us is our thinking! Why would you stop yourself from what you want? In addition, if everything is connected, this means that your passion and desire is designed to serve a greater purpose.

Look, you can desire great wealth and lots of shiny things, but those are not purpose. You weren't created to simply acquire and then leave a bunch of stuff behind. You were created for a great purpose. You have a mark to make in this great big world.

What excites you? Think about it? If you had no limitations such as income or resources, what is it that excites you that you would love to do and would make you feel good? The energy of that thing that you would do is the energy that drives dreams into reality.

Understand, that if you could imagine your dream by stripping away limitations that currently exist, you can equally strip away limitations in reality. Yes, it may take considerably more work, but if it excited you thinking about it without limitations, why wouldn't it still excite you despite limitations. You are limitless and can do anything that you set your mind to. You were created to be a creator. Only you limit you.

Passion is really cool. Passion, total crazy, head-over-heels obsession over what you want is an energy that is unstoppable. When you eat, sleep, and breath visualizing your passion, it is so alive in you that you understand that you are in the driver's seat.

Visualizing as if what you desire already is, drives action. For example, if you eat, sleep, and breath becoming a pharmacist, you would be so obsessed with becoming a pharmacist that you would know exactly what it takes to become one. You would know how many years of school, what classes to take, how much the schooling costs, and where you could go to work after school. Knowing this, you would put a plan together to start moving your dream forward.

You are limitless because you can make anything happen because you have the power to choose to decide to do so. You are limitless because you have the power to create energy that drives further creation. You are limitless because you are capable of thoughts that are pictures of things that don't exist yet. What is it that you want to create that doesn't exist in your reality yet?

Lean In – Find Discomfort

Finding comfort in discomfort is key to manifestation. As stated earlier, when doubt and fear arise, you know that you have a big, blue, hairy monster standing between you and your dream. Lean into the discomfort and doubt because, "Reality is negotiable. Outside of science and law, all rules can be bent or broken, and it doesn't require being unethical" - Timothy Ferriss.

Just because it hasn't been done before does not mean that it can't. Just because you haven't achieved before does not mean that you can't. Discomfort is a good thing! It's your alarm system and when the alarm goes off, listen! Find the source of discomfort and quickly determine your path around – remember, step to the right or step to the left when an obstacle appears directly in front of you.

"The reasonable man adapts himself to the world: the unreasonable one persists in trying to adapt the world to himself. Therefore, all progress depends on the unreasonable man" - George Bernard Shaw.

Be unreasonable to your doubts and fears. Do not bend or waver. Stand firm, as this is not the time to adapt to what you know or what exists. How can you create a new reality if you keep adapting to the current reality?

Finally, lean in to the discomfort when your purpose, that which you are most passionate about, is threatened. Each of us have a purpose, and although highly individual and unique to us, purpose connects us. "A life is not important except in the impact it has on other lives" - Jackie Robinson.

Making your mark requires leaning into the discomfort caused by opposition, even when this comes from a dark pit within you that you were unaware existed. It requires having the courage to believe in the unseen so that you can one day see it. Finally, making your mark is proof that you are limitless and meant to create and fulfill a greater purpose.

I dream of painting and then I paint my dream.

7 WHEN OUR DREAMS SEEM CRUSHED

There are times when everything that we dream about seems to come together like the instruments of a symphony, in perfect harmony and tempo. It's as if we are in perfect alignment with everything around us. We barely notice as all the pieces fall into place. It's just the way it is supposed to be. One day we look around and think, Wow! What I dreamed of actually is! It feels amazing and we float on cloud nine.

Alternatively, there are times when it seems like the whole world is against us achieving what we desire, and we feel crushed. We feel like our dreams are destroyed. It's as if we just can't seem to catch a break.

We must remember that a dream is a personal creation. Your dream cannot belong to someone else, it is yours. You might think that dreams can be shared, and that two people can share and achieve dreams together, but this is not true. Your dreams are a product of your mind that designs and gives meaning to the thoughts and feelings prescribed within you. Someone else, a spouse for example, might get excited and be in full agreement to work toward that dream, but what they see in their head, and the interpretation that they prescribe, is uniquely theirs.

Dreams are personal. This is why when we allow negative thoughts about our dreams in, we get super defensive. It feels like a personal attack, because it is, but you may be surprised who the actual attacker is! Unfortunately, it's not circumstances or other's opinions or actions that are the source of the attack – it's us. We are the culprit. We are the person sabotaging our dreams.

Just imagine how many more dreams of yours would come true if you stopped sabotaging them in your head. Self-sabotage is the killer of dreams. Is your mind working against you?

Self-sabotage is an unconscious subversion, disruption, or obstruction to hinder your own cause or endeavor. You consciously have a desired outcome, but you work against yourself unconsciously. It seems pretty ridiculous to want something and to invest the time and energy visualizing and dreaming, and then destroy it. Seems a bit counterproductive, right? Okay, a lot counterproductive.

When it seems that our dreams are crushed, this is simply a perception. This is in line with the same theory that your thoughts are your thoughts. Your dream is your dream. So how can anything or anyone crush it? Once you create it in your mind, it exists in the quantum field. With doubt, fear, and other limited thinking, your dream may become farther and farther out of your grasp, but it cannot be destroyed. It will live on in the land of possibility. Do you want to be living with your dream in your reality or in separate dimensions? The choice is yours. Ultimately, everything boils down to choice.

Think about how limitless you are. You are only limited by the boundaries that you set on your beliefs – and this happens within your mind! You have limitless ability to dream and to create. Dream crushing happens in your head.

Nobody can make you feel anything. Feelings are created by a thought that you have. If you realize how powerful your thoughts are, you'd never have a negative thought again. Okay, that's somewhat of an unrealistic statement, but if you could actually catch yourself and interrupt these negative thoughts while they are happening (which you can), then there we go- there's the secret sauce!

When you feel like your dreams are being crushed, the key is to not allow them to be. Stop crushing your dreams. Tell your stupid negative thoughts to take a flippin' hike! Seriously, when that feeling arises, stand up against those thoughts. What does that look like? Well, it somewhat looks like a crazy person standing on a street corner talking to an invisible person, but it is far more effective. Simply make an audible announcement, yes, that means out loud – "Stop! I'm not listening to you!"

Tell that manipulative, destructive, voice of doubt and deception that you simply are not going to accept what it is saying and that you are not receptive to hearing what it has to say. Done!

When we become aware of our negative thinking or counter-productive thoughts and confront them, we must remember, that they do not belong to us. They are intruders. It is important to keep this in mind, because as you can imagine, the next set of thoughts that come in are something along the lines of, "Why do I always have these negative thoughts?" or "I am not in control of what I think. No matter how hard I try, I still have negative thoughts."

Judgement has no place in our successful mindset, which is our manifestation machine. As we become aware of negative thoughts and begin confronting these thoughts as the manipulators and liars that they are, be kind and loving to yourself. You are fine. Your thinking is fine. You just have weeds growing in your garden. Remember, if you pluck off the top, the weed is going to come back. By becoming aware of the thought and stopping it in its tracks you have a chance to yank the root, but if you have ever had crab grass, you understand that sometimes you need to trace that root and all its little tentacles to finally get it out. Weeding takes consistency, attention, patience, and most important, self-love.

Fine, you say, I can be kind and loving and non-judgmental, but what about when everything that you have worked for suddenly falls apart? Believe me, I get it. You can spend months and years putting all the pieces into place, you can have invested time, money, energy, and your soul, and then it all disintegrates right in front of your eyes. Then what?

Are you ready for a shocking answer? Your dream is still there. Nothing has been crushed or disintegrated. It hasn't been destroyed and vanished off the face of the planet. It's alive and well. It just doesn't look like what you hoped it would look like at that moment. Would you try to reach into the mirror to fix your messy hair? No, you'd do what you can with your two hands and a brush or comb, in your reality, not in a reflection.

We get so hung up on what we think *ought to be* or how we *think it should look* or *feel* that we totally miss out on the sheer fact that it's still there! What you currently see is just a reflection of your past and what you will see is being worked on right now. I'm telling you, once you dream up your dream, it exists. You might forget about it, but it's there, in the land of possibility, preparing for birth.

I'm sure you have seen a movie or read a story where one of the characters, for whatever reason, is invisible to everyone around them. Scrooge is a good example. No matter how hard Scrooge tries to communicate with the people that he knows so well, he cannot be seen or heard. Your dreams are like that. They are just out of your perception and view from the physical world, yelling and screaming at you to keep the faith, hold on, don't let go, it's getting ready, and you are getting ready!

Imagine your dream, like Scrooge as he watches the world without him, saying, "I'm right here. I'm right here!" You dreamed your dream. You desired it into existence. Why would you want to allow a feeling to block you from being able to see and interact with it? That's exactly what happens when you allow yourself to crush your dreams, by giving up on them.

Dream Vitality Practice

You dreams deserve to flow, uninterrupted. How we do this is we put into place a mechanism for your dreams to grow and flourish, where you interact with them daily, and allow them to naturally transcend and manifest into your reality.

Flow is a state of being in alignment with your purpose. In this state, anything is possible and within this state, is where you can accelerate the manifestation of your dreams. Keep in mind that acceleration is subjective in that time and space do not truly exist in the context of how you and I have been programmed to believe. Acceleration simply means that you are contributing to the proper care and feeding of your dreams so that they can mature and fruit into your life.

Flow is a high state of energy and vibration. Everything around you, as you know it, is comprised of energy and is ignited by vibration. The higher the state of vibration, the higher the energy. Think of a boiling pot of spaghetti. As the pot boils, the boiling water rises higher and higher until the pot boils over. This is because the molecules are expanding and at such a high energetic state, they cannot be contained unless the energy source (the flame) is reduced. Once we turn down the flame, the molecules slow down, and the boiling water subsides.

Negative thoughts are like turning the flame down. The out-of-control energy that is boiling out of you from the excitement of thinking about your dream, immediately recedes when the energy is interrupted or cut short. By integrating vibrational energy practice into your day, you can learn to sense when your energy is being impeded and you can stay in a high state of energetic flow.

This practice only takes 5-7 minutes a day and will transform your life – not just your dream manifestation engine. Vibrational healing is an age-old practice of restoring depleted energies to their natural state. The most natural way to increase vibrational energy is through the sound.

The analogy provided in the previous chapter of a high energy football game, provides a great visual for your mind of vibrational energy. As the players get close to the goal, the crowd gets excited, they get louder, you can feel the vibration, and the energy of excitement increases within you.

Similarly, at a concert, you can feel the music, coursing through your body, even with classical music. This is because sounds vibrate at a different frequency (both high and low) than the energy vibrations of soundless life (a still tree or the grass, for example). Sound is a catalyst that we can use to help us increase our vibration and become more aware and conscious of the world around us.

When we are in flow and in a high state of vibration, we become fully aware that life is not happening to us, that we are making it happen, through our interpretation of the life as it is happening through us and for us. When our vibration increases, we can take charge of the world around us and interrupt and make adjustments when things *seem* to be impeding on our dreams, or something doesn't feel quite.

Find a quiet place where you can sit, uninterrupted for 5-7 minutes. If you need earplugs because you simply do not have anywhere that is quiet, use them, just make sure that you will not be interrupted. I actually really like earplugs because you can hear more of you, which is exactly what you want.

Sit wherever and however you are most comfortable. Close your eyes. Take a deep breath in through your nose, listening to the air and feeling it against your nostrils as it goes in. As you exhale through your nose, tighten your throat so that you loudly hear the exhaling air. Repeat this 3x. Nice full, loud exhale breaths.

Next, sit quietly, breathing normally, in and out of your nose, for the next 60 seconds. Count to 60 slowly in your head. Listen intently to the sounds around you, even if you have ear plugs. Take in the sounds.

The final step about 3-4 minutes is your reset button. The first steps clear you out and the final step resets your vibration.

Sitting with your eyes closed. Smile a closed mouth smile. Grin as comfortably as possible, there is no need to hurt your face smiling too hard. With a soft, gentle smile on your face, think of something that you absolutely love to do and while you do, softly hum. There is no right or wrong pitch. This is your music, your vibration.

Stay there with the thing that you like to do, humming for about 60 seconds. Don't try to time yourself or set an alarm, just guestimate 60 seconds. Do not count out 60, focus on that wonderful feeling of that thing that you love while softly humming.

Next, shift to your dream(s). You may have one or you may have many. With the smile still on your face, hum as you think of your dream(s). Stay here for about 60 seconds.

Your final step is to shift to the feeling that you have both when you do what you love and how you will feel when you achieve your dream(s). Don't stop humming, breath as normal as possible, smiling. Stay here for about 60 seconds.

To complete the practice, take 3 nice deep cleansing breaths. In through the nose, out through the mouth – listen intently to yourself as you take these breaths. Open your eyes. You are done. Repeat daily, one time each day.

The most common complaint I hear when explaining this process to people is, "I can never sit still that long or control my thoughts. I start thinking of everything else."

My answer to that is that most people spend three to four (or more) times that amount of time, checking Facebook posts or watching television. You can totally do 5-7 minutes, without a doubt. Now, the run-away thoughts? Yes, that is common, and that is why we are shifting thoughts, telling our mind what to think, just when it's about to try to take control (60 seconds).

Additionally, by focusing on the breath, you are telling your mind what it is allowed to focus on. All the while as we are listening and telling ourselves what to focus on, we don't have the bandwidth to be judgmental, you are continually controlling the channel. If you must mentally picture your hand on a knob, fine-tuning and adjusting as unwanted thoughts come into your mind, this will help you visualize your control. You have control and can tune out anything unwanted.

Most people who regularly practice this vibrational exercise, report clearer focus, greater awareness, feel more in control, and they start seeing things that they have desired manifest. Why is this so? Because they are aligning the correct thoughts with the right energy – the pot begins to boil over because the energy vibration is so high!

The smile on your face sends a message to your brain, "Hey, I'm happy". The brain then responds by releasing endorphins, happy hormones. By engaging your neurons and the hormonal response from the smile and connecting this messaging with deliberate thoughts, while producing vibration (humming), you are igniting your flow state. Everything is working together, the quantum field and the physical world (seen and unseen) unite!

Overcoming the Temptation to Give Up

When it feels like our dreams are crushed (even though we now know that's not true), there is a tendency to want to give up. You may give up on believing, but your dreams still go on. They can't become anyone else's. They just exist in a realm of possibility. Overcoming the temptation to give up requires thought conditioning.

Just like a professional athlete, you must regularly train and condition to stay in shape and avoid muscle atrophy. What's interesting here is that we are dealing with your mind and your spirit and neither of which were created to ever give up.

Giving-up is man-made and is the equivalent of taking a completed jig-saw puzzle, breaking it apart, and mixing the pieces around. The picture still exists in the pile of mixed-up puzzle pieces, but when you look at it, it just looks like a bunch of pieces. We can't see the picture, but it's coming together.

Conditioning your mind takes regular practice. This is why it is important to become more aware of what you are thinking and guide your thinking whenever possible. Visualization is important because it helps you stay focused on what it is that you want the picture to look like.

If you have ever done a jigsaw puzzle, there are a few ways to that you can approach the puzzle to make it a bit easier. First, you sort out anything that looks like an edge piece. They are the one with a flat side. During this process, it is your goal to find the four corner pieces; this helps you to have some sort of anchor or even starting point. Once you have started, you put the puzzle box in clear view. This is what it is supposed to look like. Throughout the puzzle-making process, you keep referring back to the image.

You take a puzzle piece into your hand and try to decipher the colors, the patterns, and where it might fit into the big picture. Our thinking is the same when it comes to holding on to our dreams.

Overcoming the temptation to give-up is done by keeping the big picture in sight at all times. If you were to look at every puzzle piece individually, but to never see how they interlink and connect, you would become overwhelmed. Just know that your dream is like a big jigsaw puzzle. Keeping focused on the big picture and what it looks like, rather than each of the pieces, will help exercise your dream manifestation muscles.

Just like when you get a serious workout and your body gets tired, you need to give your body a chance to refuel and recuperate, similarly as we are exercising our manifestation muscles, we can get exhausted. It can seem like you have been wanting and seeking that dream for forever. You may have worked hard at preparing yourself for opportunities and getting ready for its fruition, and it just never seems to come.

Just remember, brokenness is often the road to breakthrough. It's one step beyond that breaking-point when impossible becomes possible. To breakthrough to the other side – one step beyond – you've got to breakthrough any and all doubt.

There is a firmness and rigidity in dream manifestation. The only flexibility of our dreams resides in how our dreams will manifest, in the details of the puzzle. Our resolve on what our dream is, what it looks like, feels like, tastes like, smells like, is the only fixed point. Our dream is our fixed point.

This doesn't mean that your dream, as originally dreamed cannot expand or grow. This simply means that we must become unwavering in our belief that what we want is possible and that the picture in our mind, will indeed come to be.

A sticking point is that we often give way too many details that are not important or dilute an even better end result than we ever could have imagined. If we dream of finding our soul mate or true love, for example, and provide the universe with a specific person, it is only our perception that a specific person is the *only* option.

Get Out of the Weeds

Have you even wanted something, a gift or an end result, only to be completely blown away by what you got because it way exceeded your expectations? This is because we limit what is possible based on what we know. If we would just step aside for a moment, the universe is in the business of providing for us everything that we could ever desire – and that usually exceeds what we even know about our desires because the universe knows what's going on inside our mind, in our feelings, and in our spiritual being.

Look, the only way to enjoy the beauty of what the universe has to offer you is to get off the ground and out of the weeds. The universe is quite capable of taking all of those puzzle pieces and making a far more amazing picture than what you thought was possible. It also has the ability to provide, in fine detail, exactly what you ask for – so be careful what you ask.

To my dismay, I decided years back to tell the universe that I was sick and tired of not getting what I wanted and "this is how it's going to be." With every foul swear word that I could must up, I decided, while pissed off and crying to *demand* from the universe what I wanted, in the form of a letter.

Let me just say that when emotions such as love, and hate, frustration and excitement are linked to a request to the universe, stuff happens. Oh, and it happened all right. My letter was answered.

In fine detail, within 30 days, it materialized. My demand to the universe was right in front of me. The problem was, it was *literally* what I asked for – and then some. When I say be careful what you wish for, I mean it. If you make demands of the universe, and if you are in the weeds, it is weeds that you will get – and boy did I get WEEDS! I received choking, suffocating, life-sucking, weeds – and the eradication process was long and painful. The life lesson from this experience, now, is with full clarity, but when I was going through *my dream life* – not so much – in fact, there was no clarity.

Does this mean that there is some evil creator, out to teach the children of this world a lesson? No, because we are the creators. Created in the image of the creator, we have been gifted free-will. I made the demand, like a spoiled child throwing herself on the ground (and I was on the ground when I wrote the letter, crying and pissed off) and screaming, "I want it now! Give it to me!" Oh, I got it all right!

We create what we desire. Everything we see is our creation. Did I create the sky? Yes, as I interpret the sky. Did you create the sky? Yes, as you interpret the sky. Does it really matter arguing over the sky, or are we wasting our thoughts judging what is? Shouldn't we get out of the weeds so that we can enjoy the beauty around us – since we create it?

Imagine yourself in the Gardens of Versailles. There are vast sweeping lawns as far as you can see. Bordering the lawns are incredible beds of flowers, shrubbery, statues, fountains, majestic trees, as well as pools of water throughout the gardens. Birds are flying above and frolicking in the bushes and bathing in fountains. Butterflies and other small insects and wildlife interact with the natural splendor of the space. The garden is breathtaking.

As you sit under a tree, you spot a small patch of weeds. You can't take your eyes off of it and you wonder how they got there, why they are there, and how did the groundskeepers miss such an obvious patch of weeds? You are completely distracted and irritated by the weeds.

Meanwhile, the garden is still as beautiful as ever, and life energy is bursting around you, but you are abhorred by the weeds. After some time, irritated, you leave the gardens. As the sun sets on the gardens, a whole new scene exists, but you do not know that, for you were so concerned with the weeds, that what was going on around you, and what was yet to come, was blocked from your view. You didn't experience the beauty of your current reality because you were so hung up on the details in the weeds.

Your dreams are your beautiful creation and they will come, but don't miss today and the beauty of it because you choose to get hung up on the details of how you believe things should be. Don't cut your dreams short.

The future belongs to those who believe in the beauty
of their dreams.

8 BELIEVING AND ACCEPTING

Manifesting your desires is not a hocus pocus, woo-woo, way out there, bit of mumbo-jumbo. Manifestation, means an appearance or a sign of something existing or happening. To believe that we can manifest what we desire need not be so far-fetched, but rather, our right and our job as creators. It should be far more out of the ordinary not to manifest what we desire than what we do.

It's strange how just the term *manifesting of dreams,* can get so many strange looks and stir so much disbelief. I believe that this has to do with a misunderstanding of dream manifestation in the first place.

Manifesting your dreams is not sitting on the couch with a bag of chips and reciting some magic spell or repeatedly chanting for something to come into existence. Manifestation is the practice of creation from concept through inception and beyond. It's not like we think that Steve Jobs, Albert Einstein, or the Wright brothers were out of their minds for believing in this concept, but for some reason, when you and I talk about it, it all of a sudden is *way out there* kind of thinking.

Before you could ride a bike or swim, you likely had a desire to do so. Or, like my eldest daughter, you were forced to learn to swim for your own safety around the water. Regardless of whether you learned willingly (starting with a desire) or forced, you had a thought about riding the bike or swimming. This was later manifested and came into fruition.

I remember being on my first bike with the training wheels on. It was great. I wobbled side to side bouncing off one training wheel to the next, but riding all the same. The streamers from the handle bars flapped in the wind as I began to gain confidence and pedal faster. Day after day I would ride around in front of the house, down the sidewalks, and in the street with my older brother.

I distinctly remember the day when my brother announced that he was going to teach me to ride my bike without the training wheels. I was five. I wasn't terribly thrilled about not having the extra wheels and I didn't know how I was going to keep the bike up, but my brother assured me that he was going to be there to hold me up. "Okay," I thought, he was going to hold me up.

I remember my brother behind me, holding on to the bar that ran across the back of the banana seat (yep, I'm aging myself here). He told me that all I had to do was pedal and he was going to run behind me holding on so that I wouldn't fall. The tree-lined street was long and straight. I had ridden my bike, with training wheels, up and down the street and sidewalks of our Glendale, California street for weeks. I was confident in my ability to ride, especially since my brother said that he was going to be holding on the whole time. I had nothing to fear. He would catch me.

As he and I started out, after the initial wobble of positioning myself on the seat and getting comfortable as I gained pedaling momentum, I thought to myself that it seemed just like having my training wheels on. I remember thinking, my brother was obviously really good at this – and then I looked back! There was my brother, standing at the end of our driveway, and I was a good 3-4 houses up the street. It turns out, he had never so much as left the front of our house. He gave me a good running launch and I was off and riding.

No, I didn't immediately take a tumble. I was totally excited that I was doing it! I was riding all by myself. No training wheels! I seem to remember wondering if stopping or turning was going to be a problem, but if it was, I don't seem to remember. So, I obviously lived, and it wasn't memorable enough to keep in my memory bank.

Sometimes our belief systems need training wheels for a bit. We need to gain the confidence that *we can* so that when we realize that *we are,* we can rejoice in the momentous occasion. Believing shouldn't be so difficult, and for some it comes far easier than others. I think that I'm one of those that holds quite a bit of belief in my abilities, but I have found that sometimes I've needed to leave my training wheels on for just a bit longer.

One such time was when I was somewhere around three years old. I was definitely a water baby. Get me around a pool and I wanted in. My grandparents owned a pool company in Palm Springs when I was growing up, so I was always around pools. I loved going with my grandpa on his pool routes and meeting up with the uncles at their morning meeting at the Westward Ho on the main drag through town. I'd always sneak in a swim. I swam in more Hollywood stars pools in my early years, just because I could.

My love for the water, like many small children who think they have everything figured out and can do it themselves, caused me to have a false sense of confidence in my ability to swim. Never having swam without my big puffy life vest, one day I believed that I could swim on my own without the restrictive orange beast. I was given the green light by my parents and grandparents to go on in the pool without my vest. Tough love, I'm telling you. I remember stepping off the step in the shallow end of the pool and immediately going under, sinking like a lead weight. Just as quickly as I sank, a hand came down and yanked me out. I still needed my training wheels, but I believed that I was ready. It wasn't long after that, I was swimming on my own. I was determined to part ways with that big orange vest. I'm telling you, life vests have come a long way since I was a kid.

The point to these childhood memories is that we get what we are ready to receive. Training wheels play an essential role in helping us to build the skills necessary to ride a bike. We learn about pedaling slow and fast, about making turns and braking. We learn the fine art of starts and stops and the wobbles of finding balance. We gain confidence as we practice our skills.

For me, as I was learning to swim, my false confidence came from my vest. I didn't know just how much more I needed to prepare without the vest. I wasn't ready to take off the vest and swim on my own. I needed to develop my swimming skills.

How We Believe

Was I naïve in thinking that I was ready to swim? Perhaps. I didn't see why I couldn't. All I knew was that the vest was bulky and in the way. My brother and sister and aunt could all swim without a vest, so why couldn't I? I saw it as limiting. This was my belief – and it was true. The vest did limit my movement. It also limited the chance of me drowning.

Going under did not make me stop swimming. Instead, I agreed to strap the vest back on and got right back in the pool; that is after I coughed half the pool out of my lungs. It also sent a message to my parents that it was time to start helping me learn the skills necessary to swim, because I was determined to swim without the vest. My belief was strong and in no time, just like riding the bike, I was going at it solo.

So why is it that some of us have stronger beliefs in ourselves than others? Why are some people fearless? Or are they really? And how do our beliefs form?

Let's me start by saying that there is no simple way to answer these questions to encompass every unique being on this planet. We are all created as unique versions of us and then we become influenced. What we believe is influenced from before the time we are born. In the womb, you begin to experience your world.

As a first-time parent I would put headphones on my belly and play Beethoven to my son. I would read Macbeth aloud, hoping to influence a child prodigy. Although he's quite sharp, I wasn't quite able to manipulate his brain in the manner that I thought I could. He was already great as he was. What I hadn't considered were all of the other hours in the day that I wasn't trying to manipulate his unborn experience.

My conversations with other people, my surges of stress emotions, fears, happiness, my heartbeat, digestion, the sounds of the world, these were all things that he was experiencing – and I thought a bit of Beethoven once a day was going to make all the difference in the world. To my credit, he loves music, and he has a really eclectic mix of genres.

If you had overly cautious parents that made sure that you never bumped your head or fell down, it's likely that you developed a more cautious outlook on life. If your parents let you jump the neighbor's car with your bike, as long as you didn't come home wanting cash for a repair, you likely became more of a risk-taker or have a dare-devil side to your playtime.

Ask any parent of multiple children and they will tell you how different each baby was from each other. That's because we are supposed to be. With this uniqueness, how we internalize our world and experiences, is also custom, just for us. How we form beliefs is based on our perceptions, basic wiring, and external influences.

A belief boils down to a choice. Can I jump the neighbor's car with my bike? If I have a thought that yes, I can, I have chosen to accept that this is something that I can do.

Did any of us think that we couldn't walk when we were toddlers? I doubt that you can remember, but we didn't have much prior experience in our way to stop us from doing it. So, we scooted and crawled and then started pulling ourselves up on the furniture. We then had a parent, sibling, other family member, or family friend coax us on to try to walk.

"Come here," with arms out stretched, we attempted to take a step and boom, down we went. Or we took one solid step and were met with, "Wow! Look at you, little walker!"

Needless to say, we took many tumbles and practiced and built the skills and the muscles necessary to walk. All the while gaining confidence in our ability that we could. Although we don't recall that early thought, it existed. It may not have even been in the language you speak today, because it was a process of your thinking, and it became ingrained as an absolute – I will do this. Have you ever tried arguing with a toddler not to do something? Pretty futile thing to do.

As we grow and become more conscious of our thoughts, we accept far more of what others believe into our own belief systems. We adopt a hybrid version of beliefs, which we begin to refine right before our teen years and continue to refine thereafter. It is other's beliefs and influences from our experiences, coupled with other's experiences and stories that shape our beliefs and our acceptance of these beliefs as ours. Unfortunately, other's beliefs do not always ring true inside of us.

Have you ever proposed an idea to your parents or a friend, just to be told why your idea won't work? Imagine being Steve Jobs and being told that "That whole computer thing is just crazy talk. Who would actually need a computer in their house?" This seems crazy to even think about, but we are confronted with other's beliefs in this way all the time. It becomes our norm.

So why is it then that people like Steve Jobs can believe so strongly, despite opposing beliefs? Simple, choice. Why do we believe what others tell us? Yes, you guessed it, choice. Everyone is different in the way they decide which and whose thoughts that they are going to believe. Sometimes it even boils down to mood. There is no formula or algorithm as to the reason for one person choosing to accept and formulate a belief and another to not buy it. It's a personal decision, and simply put, if it doesn't feel good and doesn't fit, they don't choose to accept that thought to become their belief.

Yes, this is overly simplistic, but that is the basic truth of how beliefs work. I accepted that my brother was going to be behind me holding on. I had ridden my bike lots of times with the training wheels on. He assured me that I wouldn't fall. I chose to accept that belief. I could have chosen to get off the bike and refuse to take part in his experiment, but instead I chose to believe what he told me. Now, he was a big fat liar, and I'm glad for that, because he helped me gain the confidence in my ability to ride the bike without training wheels, but the point is that I chose to accept a belief that I could ride under the conditions that he stated.

How many times have you chosen not to believe that you could ride without your training wheels? Why? What was holding you back was a fear that it might not work out as planned. But what if you simply accepted the belief that you could, knowing that the entire process was skill building?

Take off Your Training Wheels

We can stop ourselves from believing even before we even get a chance to finish Imagineering our dreams. We cut ourselves short because we choose not to accept a belief that we are limitless. Look folks, people have flown to the moon, gone from rags to riches, designed, engineered, and built structures that were thought to be impossible. There is no limit to what can be dreamed and what can be achieved, but it all starts with accepting a belief.

Believing in what's possible might even be a stretch for you at first. My suggestion is that you practice with your training wheels for a bit. If you had no limitations and were guaranteed success, you'd believe much differently. You would stop considering if someone else has done it before. You would stop considering that you don't have all the resources (yet). You would stop beating yourself up that your idea is lame and so are you just for thinking that whatever it is that you desire is possible to achieve.

Do you think God sat back and said, "You know this heaven and earth thing, nobody's done it before;

I'm not sure if I can really do this." But what happened? "In the beginning God created the heaven and the earth" (Gen 1:1). "And God saw everything that he had made, and behold, it was very good" (Gen 1:31).

I imagine God sitting back and saying, "Dang! That's pretty awesome!" I imagine a big satisfactory smile while looking around and nodding.

We are created in the image of God as creators. We create our lives as we interpret the world around us. We create other little humans. We create things from our thoughts. This is creation and you were born into it to create. Why on earth do you want to believe that you cannot? Evidence of creation is all around you.

Do you have a job? For arguments sake, let's say yes. Before you got the job, you had a thought. "I want a job." You decided on what job that you would apply for and you pursued it. You chose to accept a belief that you wanted the job. You then chose to believe that you were capable to apply for the job. You likely had a job interview or some sort of vetting process that you had to go through to get the job, so you had to choose what you would say to help influence the belief of the hiring manager that you were the best person for the job. Everything you did to get the job, you created, through a belief.

Now, have you ever received something that you never thought that you would receive? Maybe it was something that you wanted, but didn't really believe that it was achievable, but you ended up with it anyway? That too was your creation.

We live in this crazy universe that just wants to give us our desires. Even when you have your training wheels on and start putting out there what you would like to have, without fully believing yet, you are still putting into motion the great quantum realm of creation – the realm of possibility.

Begin with your training wheels on. Understand that you can kick into motion the creation of your dreams without having a clue how it could actually happen; and that's actually good, not getting stuck in the details, because as we learned earlier, you may get so stuck in the weeds that you miss out on some pretty darned amazing experiences.

I believed that I could swim without the vest. Although I wasn't ready just yet, I was right. I learned to swim because I believed that I could. I needed the training wheels just a bit longer. Your dreams will transpire when you are ready. When the resources are put into place, the skills, the people, the circumstances, the things, when they are aligned, it's going to happen – but it all starts with believing. If it makes you feel wobbly, use the training wheels for a bit. Let me explain how.

Get into the practice as introduced in the prior chapters of gaining awareness of what you are thinking when you are afraid. It's okay, leave the training wheels on as you practice this a bit. What you are going to find is that as you begin visualizing what you want, you are going to start allowing yourself to believe.

Accepting the possibility of achieving your dreams starts by practicing the art of awareness, and this begins to create certainty of the inevitable. The only thing standing between impossible and possible is the "im" in the front. In other words, tell yourself as you are practicing becoming aware of fears, doubt, and I can't, "*Im* the only thing coming between my dreams and them becoming possible." Be certain of this, because it is true.

There is a whole lot of head work to do in this art of believing thing, so that you can manifest your dreams. We've got to undo and re-engineer your thinking, dissecting out the beliefs that are not serving you and replacing them with new beliefs that you have accepted as your truth.

The art of accepting is in unconditionally accepting without judgement, what it is that you want. Your new belief is your truth and nobody else's. Your dreams are your private property and for no one to judge, not even you.

Creation is not meant to be judged, but accepted and lived. To live your dreams is to accept and to believe in them. The belief in the unseen as if you are awaiting the arrival of a special guest into your home that you have not seen for ages.

Anticipation of your dream, solidifies your belief as it is a fully accepted thought that you are awaiting its arrival – it's manifestation. This is when the training wheels come off and you ride solo without even realizing that you are doing so. It happens so magically fast that you, like me, will look back and say, "Hey, I did it!"

The Key to Accepting

If acceptance is the binding element of beliefs, what is the key to getting to acceptance in the first place? You want, you desire, you dream, yet you don't know how it will ever happen. Or maybe there is something deep down inside, a belief planted by someone through an action or statement, that maybe you don't deserve whatever it is you desire. You certainly wouldn't be the first person with emotional baggage.

Even if you don't recognize it as emotional baggage, let's look at this because the emotion is extremely important here. Every result in our life is the result of an action or inaction (and arguably, an inaction is an action as well). Every action or inaction is a direct result of a thought that you have and an attached feeling.

As we interpret our world, through our senses, our mind is hard at work making sense of what is happening. From smells, to sights, to sounds, and physical sensations, we take in and interpret the world around us, by thinking. Some of this thinking happens automatically and some is on purpose as we are consciously aware of what we are thinking.

Through the simple experience of our sheer being, we are continually being barraged by the influential environment. Statements or actions by others or circumstances in our environment are interpreted as pleasant, unpleasant, indifferent, and so on, and filed away in our memories. Like photographs being stored away, the influences become a part of our internal file system and a feeling is attached to each. Our emotional baggage is the product of our filing away absolutely everything we encounter.

The more emotionally charged our experiences, the heavier the associated feeling to the picture within. So, for every thought that you actively are having or have translated subconsciously or automatically, there is an associated feeling. We act and react based on our feelings. The feeling comes as a result of the thought. When we act, we get results. So, inaction, as I was saying, is also an action, because you choose not to take action, but you still have the same conclusion to this cycle, a result.

If a negative subconscious thought in relation to your worthiness exists because it was a seed planted by someone else, you may not believe that you actually deserve your dream. This is why it is so important to become aware of any negative feelings that we have relative to pursuing our dreams, whether it is doubt, insecurity or fear. Bringing these untruths out and exposing them to the light will help you in achieving the confidence that you need in accepting the belief that you can – and where exactly does this confidence come from? Certainty.

If I asked you if you were 100% guaranteed not to fail and to succeed at what it is that you want, would anything hold you back from pursuing that dream? Heck no! You would be all over that dream like white on rice. Certainty is the key to acceptance and its partner is confidence.

Certainty is an amazing feeling. It is unwavering. It is confident and assertive. It is, and there are no ifs, ands, or buts – certain just is. If you are certain in your desire for your dream, you can certainly become certain that you can achieve your dream.

Remember, if you can see it in your head, you can create it to see it with your eyes, but you must be certain that you can do this. Time doesn't matter. Time and space are irrelevant in the quantum world. There are no barriers and there are no parameters outside of those that you construct in your head.

Whether you think you can, or you can't, you are correct, so choose to be certain, because it is a much better feeling than uncertainty and confusion. Certainty, when attached to our desires and dreams, is like nitrous oxide (NOS) for a street racer, it gives you that blast past everyone else. Certainty is a super-boost for your confidence, which in turn boosts the intensity of desire and the frequency that you are transmitting to the world and universe around you.

Think about the energy in a concert or high-powered event. Imagine the energy at something like a Tony Robbins sort of super-charged event. What gets everyone so pumped at these events is the high vibrational frequency of the energy. It's addictive and you want to be a part of it. Would you rather sit and chat with Eeyore from Winnie the Pooh or Tony Robbins? Okay, even if Tony is too amped for your blood, you probably would still be far more attracted to a positive conversation than a doom and gloom conversation. Why? Energy.

Certainty creates a completely different energy within us, that exudes from us. If you are certain that you are going to be promoted, you act different. Again, why is this? What did we discuss? Because every action, voluntary or involuntary is a direct result of a thought and a feeling. When you are certain, you act different, and you get different results.

Certainty will solidify the acceptance of your belief and will serve as a catalyst for the manifestation of your dream. Remember, time is irrelevant. Do not place constraints on creation. It will come to you when you are ready – when you ARE ready, not when you THINK that you are ready.

Dreams come true as we allow the opportunity of the dream to enter our life, and not a minute too soon. Once alignment between what you are thinking, feeling, accepting to believe to be your truth, your future has been achieved as you stand firm in certainty, things just happen – mountains move.

What is it that you want? What is it that is standing between you and your dreams? It could just be that you need to find room in your emotional baggage for certainty. Just as darkness cannot exist where there is the slightest glimmer of light, doubt and uncertainty cannot exist where there is certainty.

Be certain in what you desire and that you are the only one and the most qualified to be you. Why would you accept someone else's belief that contradicts what you desire to be your destiny? You hold the key to accepting new beliefs that you can and that you will achieve your dreams. Certainty will help you unleash your full potential wherein you will be unstoppable, and your dreams will be inevitable.

9 AFFIRMATION

There is a beauty in knowing. How many times have you made a statement like, "If I just knew for sure," or, "If I just knew how it would turn out"? What would knowing have done? Provided you with a sense of assurance and security? But again, aren't these feelings? And aren't assurance and security based on confidence and certainty?

Shouldn't you really be asking for a new feeling? Shouldn't you really be asking for confidence? Perhaps your statement should be, "If I just had more confidence." Now we are talking!

If you just had more confidence and certainty, then you could believe? As we discussed, yes, confidence is what shores up and nails into place your acceptance of a belief. Let's now look at the final piece of the bridge that we are building between your dream and manifestation of that dream – knowing.

Knowing comes from assurance and feelings of affirmation that what you desire will truly happen.

Think of affirmation in this way – a firm action. The definition is the action or process of affirming something or being affirmed. It's a declaration, a statement, an assertion, proclamation, pronouncement, or attestation to the universe. It is emotional support or encouragement.

Remember, your thoughts create a feeling which leads to an action and a result. If you have a firm, steady action based on the thought that you are having to support the belief and feeling associated with that belief, there is only one result possible – your dream, manifested.

Affirmation is a firm commitment to the belief, and is the bridge between certainty of the dream and what is to become. Affirmation is a beacon, signaling the dream to its destination to take root and be planted. Affirmation is your proclamation – this is mine! I deserve this dream which I desired, and I created, and therefore it belongs to me.

Our destiny is in our affirmation, the firm declaring action of our truth, the experience that we desire. Destiny in the traditional definition is fate. The word has almost been given a bad rap over the years as if fate is negative. I believe that this is because the full definition of destiny, which is the events that will necessarily happen to a particular person or thing in the future, or the hidden power believed to control what will happen in the future, fate, have been tainted to take on a meaning that we have a fixed path. No, our destiny is what we call forth and affirm. We are destined to receive. We are not destined to receive only what someone else wants us to receive.

The "hidden power" believed to control what will happen in the future is inside of you. Your thoughts.

This is why forced beliefs or beliefs accepted subconsciously don't work for us. Nobody can think for us. When a belief doesn't fit, it manifests – it's like diarrhea of the soul – you can't hold it back and it can feel very uncomfortable.

When we are in agreement with our dreams and our authentic self, affirmation of these truths, proclamation of what is rightfully ours, feels great! Affirmation isn't just some silly positive statement and positive thinking. Affirmation is a powerful tool that anchors what's coming to what is. With every tool, you must learn to use it.

Understanding Universal Law

Why are affirmations so important if we have certainty? I mean, it seems reasonable that if I believe something with utmost confidence and certainty that I will certainly achieve it, right? Well, certainty is only part of the equation.

Certainty brings about a confidence which helps you shake off negativity, but affirmation helps direct your subconscious mind which is continually working. Something that you may not pick up through conscious thought and awareness, that darned super-efficient subconscious mind of yours might catch. To ensure that you guide your mind in a way that serves you, we practice affirmation thinking.

Our thoughts, whether conscious or unconscious are stories and descriptions that we are telling ourselves. We tend to live out what we are thinking. So, if consciously you are stating that you are certain, but subconsciously a doubt still exists, it is an affirmation that will override the doubt. Affirmation shines light into the darkness and weakens any footholds on doubt.

Many are familiar with, or have at least heard about the law of attraction. For those unfamiliar with this universal law, it is basically that we create what we desire and that anything that we can think of, we can create in our lives. Under this premise, it would be easy to assume that if we look in the mirror every morning and repeat the same words over and over again, that something will change our lives. There is truth in this, but habitual negative thought patterns must be interrupted to make significant changes in our lives.

Whatever we repeatedly and consistently do becomes a habit. The same is true for what we tell ourselves, as long as we believe what we are saying. When we state positive affirmations over and over, this can help us shift out of negative thought patterns, but as mentioned, we must believe it. And how do we do this? We connect through visualization, so that we can actually see this being a part of our life.

However, visualization is not enough, there is still one missing essential piece that is something in our daily lives that we seem to employ by default, rather than purposely focus on for our benefit – emotion. Most of our lives we segment our body, from our thoughts and from our hearts. When we do this, we separate ourselves from the power of affirmation and manifestation. There is a shift that must take place, to bring alignment back between our body, mind, and spirit as we call forth our desires into our experience.

Let's examine this concept, imagine yourself sitting in front of a mirror and saying, "I am successful." You repeat this over and over with no emotion. About half way through your little attempt to convince yourself through this chant, you begin to think about all your failures in life. Those limiting beliefs trapped in your subconscious tend to rear up at the most inappropriate times. It's like all of your failures just decide to plop themselves on the floor in front of you. As you look at each of these failures, they stare you down. From here, it goes downhill fast. Your mind disconnects fully from any possible emotional connection to your body and soul and an evil little thought pops into your mind – successful, who are you kidding? And then you give up.

The shift out of negative thought patterns requires that we become aware of the thoughts as soon as they arise. Remember, once they are exposed to the light, we have an upper hand. Our mind is in constant battle with negative subconscious baggage, as if we do not deserve happiness, so this is where affirmational thinking can bring about transformation in our lives and the manifestation of our desires.

What is really great is that affirmational thinking won't just weaken doubt, it actually, over time destroys doubt. Again, darkness cannot exist where there is light. As soon as you keep the light shining in, darkness will dissipate.

There are universal truths within the universe:

1) Love transcends all space and time
2) Space and time are irrelevant
3) Everything is energy
4) Energy in action is powerful

These truths coincide with your ability to manifest and the connection of affirmation to bring about what it is that you desire. Let's first understand a bit about this creation connection.

Our purpose for existence is not only as unique as each of us, but it is a result of our research and experience of life. We are born as researchers. We are born to inquire and to seek knowledge and understanding.

As we go through our research experience, life, we collect data. We collect data on what it is that we like, and what it is that we do not like. We have ups and downs, good and bad experiences. Contrast is one of the most important elements of your experiential research.

If something doesn't feel good inside, you gain an understanding that this is not something that you desire. There is good and bad for a reason, because during this process you are understanding more about what it is that you desire. As you learn what you desire, desire become stronger, and this is an essential part of attraction and manifestation.

Our purpose within this life, is to create the life that we desire. Although we are born alone, we don't have to do this alone and that is where experiencing love and compassion come into the equation. Just feel what love feels like when you think of it. It's warm and comforting. It can be exciting and exhilarating. If you have had a bad experience in love, you may attach more strongly to the negative emotions. Find a positive love emotion to attach to – even if it is a love for peanut butter. Feel the goodness of love.

Love for yourself, which then becomes an outward reflection toward others, increases the vibrational energy around you. Again, everything is energy and energy in action is powerful. As you increase the frequency of your vibrational energy through feelings of love for yourself, not egotistical, false love, but true, positive love and acceptance of you, you increase the quantum field of attraction. Like attracts like.

Emotions are the key to attracting life experiences. Whatever we repeatedly think and feel becomes the main component of what we live. On that same note. The power of the spoken word, energy expressed through words, and words being expressions of our thoughts, provide a powerful vibrational energy. The energy of the spoken word far surpasses that of mere thought alone as the vibrational energy through speech is increased. Think of music playing at a low volume and then turning it up until you can feel the music. It is that same concept. So, when we speak, we call into action, a firm action.

I have discussed how limiting beliefs get stuck in our subconscious, yet there are times that we don't realize the power of what we are calling forth. Whatever we repeatedly and consistently say, we will believe, even at a subconscious level.

How many things do you call into your life that you love, that contradict what you really want? I LOVE chocolate. Chocolate is one of those things that I believe that I cannot live without. Without balance within my desire for chocolate, what do I put into action? Fat. If I desire certain foods that can contribute to excess weight more than I desire fitness, my love for one thing, my focus, is calling forth fat. We don't even realize how powerful our affirming thoughts are until we pay attention to our results, negative or positive. Like attracts like. If I like chocolate more than I like a fit body, what am I going to get?

We need to stop resisting what we truly desire by focusing more so on what we do want, instead of the imbalance of what we do not. We need to increase the vibrational energy in each of the five areas of our lives, to bring alignment and balance into our affirmation to ourselves. These five areas are career, family, financial, wellness, and spirituality.

By increasing our vibrational energy in spoken words, beyond just what we are thinking, we awaken and invigorate the amazing energy of the universe that's soul desire is to give us what we want. We cannot use generic affirmational statements to call forth what we want, we must be specific, so by focusing every day on the five key areas of your life, you can call forth a more balanced alignment of manifestation energies. This also helps us to root out subconscious beliefs that are not serving us.

You wouldn't go to the doctor and sit quietly and not tell him or her what your symptoms are. And on the same note, if after staring at you, not examining you or hearing what your symptoms are, your doctor would not prescribe medication or recommendations. But what if your doctor did? Would you really expect that without examination of the problem that the prescription should work?

Affirmations are soul medicine and must be targeted at your desires. Where feelings of unworthiness exist, affirmations can be delivered in a way that your inner truth becomes aligned to the affirmational statement, negating any false negative emotions. So how do we go about delivering our much-needed soul medication?

As data collectors and researchers, our desires become apparent. Like watching the rhythm of your heart, up and down, on an EKG, life has ups and downs and the line is not meant to be flat. It is from these ups and downs of life experiences that you become aware of your desires and your dreams. You begin to crave joy, happiness, and fulfillment of good feelings.

Truth within each of us, when combined with positive emotional experiences provides us with a definition of what and who we want to be and clarity of the life that we truly desire. Once we stop trying to control everything outside of us, other's actions, other's thoughts, other's behaviors, and simply focus on what we can control, our interpretive thoughts that provide us with the feelings that we desire, we are on our way to affirming our dreams. We are able to relax and not be so resistant with limiting thoughts and beliefs. We are able to love ourselves enough to allow in what it is we truly desire. We are able to be patient, kind, and loving as we pursue our dreams. We are able to affirm our confident self and the certainty of our ability to create the life that we desire.

Affirming our Desires

As we understand how to move forward into affirmations, we need to accept our worthiness as a universal given and that happiness is not something deserved, but our birthright. With these universal truths as our foundation, we need to separate our faults, hurts, and trauma and realize that they have nothing to do with what we deserve. Past experiences and circumstances need to be separated from what we desire other than being an experiential learning device to solidify what it is that we want. The key to keep in mind is that we are here now, in this moment, and that's all that matters. Our trials give us perspective and make us warriors for what we want. Fight for it. Proclaim it with a firm action.

A firm action (affirmation) proclaiming what it is that we desire through the spoken and unspoken word, when consistently and repeatedly messaged, brings for results. Just like when you go on a diet and all you can think about is having an ice cream sundae, what will you call forth? An ice cream sundae.

Focusing on that thing that you want the most, that thing that you cannot go a day without thinking about, and affirming its destiny and place in your life is done through conscious action. There are many activities that we can do to affirm our desires, and we will introduce a few to you. We like to keep these affirmational exercises as simple as possible so that you are more likely to do them consistently. Read through the following activities and then choose one or all to apply into your daily practice. Although affirmations can be done at any time, it's best to choose a time of day where you are free from distractions that you can focus all of your energy toward affirming what you would like to manifest in your life.

Note Card Affirmation Activity

You will need 5 cards. You can either make them from sheets of paper cut down to 3 x 5" or you can purchase a pack of 3 x 5" notecards. On the top of each of the 5 cards, label one of the 5 affirmational pillar areas. You will have one card for: career, family, wellness, financial, and spiritual.

Picture in your mind what it is that you desire in each of these five areas. The first thing that pops into your mind for each area is usually your top desire. Once you have the desire in your mind, think about the feeling associated with having that desire. Is it exhilaration? Is it joy? You will write a statement that includes the feeling. For example, I am joyful thinking about my new house with the sweeping staircase or I am exhilarated thinking of driving through the countryside of Ireland.

Rather than simply stating that I am taking a trip to Ireland, I have attached a feeling of how it feels when I am there experiencing it. It feels awesome thinking about the feeling attached to the experience of living your dream and what does this do? It increases that love vibration and the energy associated with your creation. Write down the top desire that you visualized and tied an emotion to. As you write it, speak it. Remember, that words are thoughts expressed and that the vibrational power of the spoken word increases the frequency of the vibration. You have just turned up the volume, the music of your soul. Feel it pulse through you!

Repeat this visualization until you have an affirmation attached to a feeling for each of the 5 pillar areas. If you think of additional items for each or specific pillar areas, repeat the visualizing, writing, and speaking forth process for each.

The next step is to read these statements daily aloud. Allow yourself to be transported to seeing you living your desired truth, the truth that you are creating through the emotional visualization experience.

Over time you can cut out small pictures from magazines and glue then to your cards. This further enhances the imagery as you *window shop* through magazines for the image that best represents your desire.

Affirmational Journal Activity

As stated, affirmations can be performed at any time, but commitment to your responsibility in the moment is imperative. The word responsibility can be translated as your ability to respond. Not just your physical or mental ability, but your willingness to respond. By committing to your responsibility during your affirmations, you are committing to be able to respond to a firm action. This means that you are committing to take firm action, swiftly identifying and exposing any negative feelings that may arise as you affirm what it is that you want in your life.

In a seated position, begin by taking three full, deep breaths. Become aware of everything around you, the sounds, the smells, the temperature of the room, or anything distracting. Acknowledge that all of these things exist, and in your mind, pardon yourself from these things. Simply state in your head, "Distractors, excuse me, it is time to focus on my desires." This will also include any limiting thoughts that may rise up during your affirmations. If a negative thought arises during your affirmation journaling exercise, simple state, "Untruths are not welcome, I am affirming what I desire and deserve."

Relax your body and think about what you desire in your life. Think of each of the five pillar areas: family, career, wellness, financial, and spiritual. What is it that you want?

Write down in your journal the feelings associated with your desires. Be as descriptive as possible with as many feeling words as possible (joyous, wonderful, happy, blissful, exuberant, etc.). List one set of descriptive statements or phrases that describes your desire for each pillar area.

Choose one of your desires that you wrote down that you believe would bring you the greatest sense of happiness and joy if it were in your life right now. For example, if you wrote down a promotion, think about a moment during your career that you simply rocked your job – maybe you rocked it so much that you impressed yourself! With this thought in mind, take a deep cleansing breathe (in through the nose and out through the mouth deeply and slowly) and feel that feeling of success in your job, and now say the affirmation, I am fabulous in my job and I deserve my promotion. You can start by thinking this statement and then aloud. Repeat this.

Use enthusiasm instead of logic, passion instead of indifference. What this does, is turn your whole body into a vibrational energy machine, shifting every cell in your body to align with the quantum energy of creation around you. The high vibrational energy goes out as your order into the universe (into the quantum field).

Vision Boarding/Traditional and Techy Activity

Vision boarding is an age-old affirmation practice wherein, pictures and visual representations of your dreams are compiled and displayed in a place that you will see them and be reminded of them daily. Traditional vision boarding is typically done on a corkboard or in a large poster frame. Simply cut out pictures from magazines of what it is you desire and attach to the board.

There are also vision board apps to be able to compile your visions electronically so that you have them with you wherever you go. This is extremely helpful if you travel quite a bit. Another electronic method is to have your vision pictures as your computer screensaver so that the images scroll across your screen when your computer is not in use.

Although having these visual cues and reminders of your desires in constant view throughout your day is important, again, an affirmation – a firm action must have emotional energy stimulated daily for the affirmation to have sticking power. The vibrational energy of a visual reminder is much weaker than the vibrational energy of a visual reminder and an associated feeling of what living that desire would be like.

Similar to the 3 x 5" card exercise, reserve a time each day to connect the vision to the feeling and state the affirmation to send forth your highest vibrational order into the universe. Imagine yourself sitting in a restaurant with an empty coffee cup. You could sit and stare at the cup, imagining coffee in it and how great that coffee would taste and how happy it would make you feel to have that cup of coffee, but until you announce to the server walking past with the coffee pot, "I'd love more coffee please," your order didn't have as much power. Yes, eventually the server would have gotten around to you, but you wanted to increase your chance of getting what you want right away. Your proclaiming your vision board items is just the same. Announce what you want. Imagine yourself with your desired vision. Feel it. If you can feel it, all that needs to happen is for it to show up. You are almost there.

Affirming Truth

Living our desired truth is the goal of our affirmations. There are enough limiting beliefs and untruths that become lodged in our subconscious that when what our desire becomes our main focus and begins drowning out negative thought patterns, we feel invincible. Anything seems possible because it is. There are infinite possibilities and it just takes calling these out through our believing in our dreams and allowing opportunity in.

The bridge between what we want and what is lies in affirmation – proclaiming what is rightfully ours from a place of surety and certainty builds confidence in our divine right to create the life of our dreams. Dreams do come true, we simply need to believe enough that we allow the firm action to take place.

What has traditionally been believed by society throughout the ages is that miracles are only the manifestation of divine intervention. This has become a widely common belief and therefore anything that transcends our understanding is therefore of God, of an unknown force, or a miraculous anomaly. What if I were to tell you that miracles should be expected. At least if we are considering miracles to be something that we call forth through faith and belief and persevering thought.

To believe that we are created by a mighty creator, in the image of the creator, and not be creators ourselves is irrational. So, we can call our manifestations miracles or dreams coming true, but regardless, they should be expected, because we are mighty creators. If we are not creating, we should be concerned. If we are not manifesting desired results we should take notice. Are we getting in the way? Are we not ushering in what we desire? Are we not living our purpose?

The truths that are a part of our every cell understand all. If we can just get out of our own way, by understanding that the ups and downs of life, every negative statement and every positive one serves a purpose – to drive us closer to our desired state. From our desired state we can live our highest calling. We are composed of truths and surrounded and permeated by universal truths. When we allow our truths to be affirmed, we call forth our birthright as creators.

We are beautiful, miraculous beings, formed from molecular energies expanding and multiplying. We are not meant to be stagnant. We are meant to continually expand in knowledge, understanding, truth, and love. We are meant to live a fulfilling life that we desire, not one we simply endure. We have the power to change everything through a thought.

The power to change our world through thought is illustrated throughout humanity. From harnessing fire as cavemen, to operating spacecrafts into the galaxy. What we can see in our minds can become tangible and visible with our eyes. If you can dream it and believe it, you can live it and be it. We must expect nothing less than our ability to transcend what seems possible, pushing beyond the range or limits of comprehension and possibility.

The truth of our dreams lies not in how they come, but that they will, and this must be affirmed. Affirmation is like a suspension bridge, tall, stately, and supported through certainty, confidence and belief. Affirmation is a firm action to the manifestation of dreams.

Go after your dream no matter how unattainable others think it is.

10 YOUR ACTION PLAN

As a life coach, helping my clients get clear on their goals and developing an action plan to achieve what it is they want, is something I do quite often. But one thing that I am not fond of is rigidity in the method that is used in helping my clients get from Point A to Point B, or should I say, helping them guide themselves from Point A to Point B. This is the same philosophy that I suggest you use in developing your action plan to manifest your dreams.

Sure, there have been activities, practices, and small rituals that you can employ that have been suggested throughout this book, that may help you stay on track and focused, and help you break through the barriers of negative and limiting beliefs along your journey, but keep in mind that rigidity may pose a potential barrier. If we keep the plan fluid enough to roll with any needed shifts, we have built success into your action plan. The point is that these recommendations are to help drive home the most important message of this entire book – NEVER GIVE UP ON YOUR DREAMS! The goal is to get you on that path!

If you can dream it, you can make it happen. Do you want it? How bad? Then fight for it, and let's come up with a game plan for you to fire up your manifestation engine by supercharging your belief in you and your abilities, and let's do this!

The Steps

There are seven steps involved in the manifestation of your dreams: Deciding, Believing, Committing, Focusing, Expecting, Affirming, and Receiving. Developing a game plan that is fluid enough to go with the flow but certain enough to be confident in the inevitable outcome is vital.

Deciding

WHAT - Your very first step is to determine what the heck it is that you want. This is that absolutely huge, audacious thing in your life that you want to manifest more than anything. There may be subcomponents of this, but those are not important right now. This is the BIG ONE. For example, perhaps you have a dream to become a millionaire. That is your big, audacious goal. Decide what star you are shooting for and aim for it.

You are going to write a game plan for this dream. Keep in mind that this is different from your visualization and affirmation activities, but they will be related and aligned. With this big huge dream, we are going to develop a game plan and you are going to have some concrete actions and goals assigned to this.

I suggest that you get a small notebook. This can be an inexpensive spiral bound type of notebook. The little composition books that you used in school also work really well for this. You will be writing quite often in this, so make sure it is an actual notebook or composition notebook so that everything is in one place and you can refer back to it.

Once you have made the decision on what that big, crazy dream is, write it down. You don't have to write it in any particular wording. We aren't using psychology to trick your brain here, we are getting laser focused. Focus is going to come farther down your seven-step list here, but in this step you need to state what you want.

"I want to be a millionaire."

Does that just mean one million? Does this mean consistently, year after year? If so, let's get specific. *I'd like to generate a minimum income of one million dollars a year.* Is that before or after taxes? Gosh darn it. I just don't let up, do I? Okay, okay. *I'd like to generate a minimum income of one million dollars per year after taxes.*

That's more like it!

What I need is for you to really drill down on what it is that you want. For example, you don't want to have a goal like, "I want to be successful," or, "I want success." These are so vague and subjective that they lack meaning. It's highly likely you don't even know what that means, so how is the universe supposed to know. Seriously, if one man's trash is another man's treasure, what is success to one person could be failure to another. Be specific.

HOW- Following what it is you want, you are going to write how you want to feel as a result of achieving your dream. This feeling is in future tense. You are going to be imagining the feeling of living with the dream. What is it like. Write a really descriptive statement about how it feels.

WHY- The next thing that you are going to write is what it means to have your dream. This is likely going to be the hardest one for you to write. This is your why. Take your time. What this does is grounds your dream into your purpose.

Remember that your purpose on this planet is based on your research and the data that you have collected over the course of your life as to what you like and don't like. Every up and down, joy and hardship has driven you to a point of where you are today with the decision that you want this one thing more than anything else on this planet. What is this reason. This is your purpose statement, so work on this as long as you need to. The clearer you get, the easier it will be to manifest into your life exactly what it is that you want.

Believing

If you believe it will work, you will see opportunities. If you believe it won't you will see obstacles. The thing with our dreams is that we see them in our head, so the only thing standing between our dreams and their manifestation is in our head.

Limiting beliefs, doubt, fear, and wanting to give up, this is the constant battle that will be on throughout the course of your dream manifestation.

Many teachers of manifestation talk about assigning specific timeframes to our dreams and goals, but why limit the universe? What if what the universe wants to deliver is one hundred times better than what you stated that you wanted? But you wanted it by a certain date? Do you really want a half-baked dream? Or can you wait?

Remember the universal law, time and space are irrelevant. Sure, it may seem to you like a specific time is best, because that's what you think and that's what you desire, but time isn't really a thing in the universal realm. What I'm trying to say is stop getting hung up on this time thing. Consistently have faith and believe in your dream. Never ever, ever give up on your belief, even when it's hard – especially when it's hard – no matter how long it takes.

In your dream notebook, write why you choose to believe in your dream and why you deserve your dream.

Write down 3 things that you will do each and every week that will help you keep the faith and keep your belief in your dream.

Finally, anytime something from your subconscious comes against your belief, write down the opposite in the belief section of your notebook. For example, if someone says, "There is no way that you will become a millionaire." You write, there is every way possible that I will become a millionaire.

These flipping statements help your subconscious to recognize that for every negative statement, there is a positive truth statement that exists. The negative statement is not an absolute truth and is exposed for the superficial "fake news" that it is.

Committing

Commitment is what transforms a hope into reality.

Think about a time that you wanted to do something, and you hesitated. What was in that pause? What stopped you from going all in and believing in what you want – and more importantly, in you?

Questioning, "Should I?" can become a derailing question. To get past the derailment of the pause, we must become focused on what we want so that we can go all in.

The better question when opportunity arises is, "Do I want this?" There is no time for "Yes, but…. (usually followed by, "I'm not sure how."), but instead, a simple Yes or No.

If yes, it's time to go all in! If no, move on and look forward, never second guessing the decision. It takes being all in to be successful at anything.

Look at life as if it were a game of poker, when you are confident and ready to receive and win, you are all in, and when you don't see yourself winning, you fold. You have to decide, yes, this is the hand, and you put your chips on the table and bet on yourself.

When a surfer decides to catch that killer wave, it's time to be all in. One hesitation, and the moment is gone to ride that perfect wave. Paddle hard in preparation as you see the wave swelling, and say yes, I'm riding this wave out.

What if the wave turns out to be a dud? What if the hand that is dealt is not a winner? Are you going to go over and over in your head for the next week, month, year, or decade how "if you wouldn't have"? How is that going to move you forward?

Likewise, we can't "sort of" decide to catch the wave or make that bet. We must commit and that all starts in our head. "I'm going all in."

"There's a difference between interest and commitment. When you're interested in doing something, you do it only when it's convenient. When you're committed to something you accept no excuses; only results" -Kenneth Blanchard.

Deciding to go all in starts with saying yes, despite not knowing how. There may be skills that you build along the path to ready you when opportunity arises, and then there may be skills that you gain along the way of building that dream.

If you want to learn to surf, you are ready to go all in with every promising wave. You position yourself on the board as you begin to paddle into the flow, and then what? All in time!

As you make your way onto the wave, you jump to your feet – and then kersplash! You are down. Then what? You ready yourself for the next opportunity to go all in! When you commit, you keep at it until you are finally successful, gaining additional knowledge and skill along the way.

Instead of "Should I?" ask yourself "Do I want it?". If you want it, it's time to go all in.

If you are ready to make real change, it's time to change your thinking to get different results. Going all in is a commitment to yourself, a belief in you, and what you want.

If you can see it in your head, you can make it appear in front of your eyes, but you can't just have ordinary thoughts and take ordinary actions. No! You have to think in an extraordinary new way, breaking down barriers in your thinking that stop you in your tracks. Hold fast to your dreams. They are worth fighting for.

Your attitude determines your direction. It's time to get what you want. It's time to GO ALL IN!

Your commitment to this dream. What does that look like? In your journal, write, *My Commitment to My Dream.* Every week, once a week, you are going to write a sentence or two stating what action(s) that you plan to take this week (within the next 7-day period) that will show your commitment to your dream.

If you have no clue what it takes to become a millionaire and you have no clue what kind of job or business that you could be in to become a millionaire, you may set an action goal for the week of researching how many millionaires have made their millions. The thing to be mindful of is we often bite off more than we can chew as we think we need to dedicate hours and hours to show how serious we are.

Instead focus on quality over quantity. Lay out action items that are meaningful. Chances are, the more passionate you are as you start taking steps consistently as you keep your dream alive, you are going to invest more and more time, but keep everything in bite size manageable chunks for commitments each week. Set yourself up for success. Easy wins keep you motivated as long as they are meaningful activities that will move you forward.

Focusing

Knowing exactly what you want and staying committed to a belief in something that you can only see in your head requires laser focus. Your focus needs to be so intense that it is burned into your mind and you see it when your eyes are open, closed, and when you are awake and asleep. You live it, you breath it, you dream it, you feel it, and it is every part of your existence.

Your focus keeps your dream alive. It is the driving force and energy that breaths life into your dream each and every day.

Think of a professional athlete training for the Olympic games. That athlete is only focused on one thing, preparing to win. There is no, "If I win." No, these athletes train to win. They train to be the winner. They don't train for second or third place. They train to win. Laser focus.

You aren't believing "if." You are believing "when." You aren't believing for a limited time, you are believing through manifestation. Your focus cannot waver. You must keep your eye on the goal at all times. This means that you are going to have to become really good at spotting obstacles and challenges that might cause you to head trip.

Keep your dream in the main stream. Talk about it, vision board it, affirm it, live it. Imagine coming back from an amazing event, vacation, or concert – what do you do? You talk about it. You show people pictures. You SHARE your experience. Why? Because it lit you up and you want to keep that light alive! Your dreams are the same way. Share them – frequently – as if they were the most amazing vacation getaway EVER. Share the feeling. It's contagious and people are going to want to help you as well as cheer you on to success!

Headwork in visualizing and planning is NOT senseless daydreaming. People like Elon Musk do this regularly. How do you come up with a vision to go to Mars without putting a lot of thought into this and thinking about the details of people and organizations that he might need to learn about and get to know?

This is just the beginning of finding clarity and living the life of your dreams, but there has to be a beginning if you ever want to cross the finish line – and we are all going to cross a finish line. The question is, will your finish line be that of the rat race or the finish line to the life that you have always dreamed of?

How will you stay focused? So far you have decided, believed, and committed through specific actions that you have and will take. What does focus look like to you?

This big, hairy dream, how are you going to keep the passion, excitement, and fire burning for it? What are steps that you can plan to stay focused?

Affirmations.

Your daily affirmations on all of the supporting elements to your dream. Each of your five pillar areas will likely be linked to your big dream. If for example your big dream is to become a millionaire, it is highly likely that your career and financial visions are aligned with your big goal. If not, and your other dreams have no connection to your big goal, you will develop a sixth vision card, add this to your journal, or add this to your vision board. This sixth dream will become a part of your visioning and affirmation process.

Remember that the most important element of the visioning and affirmation process is the emotional connection as if you already have it. For your big dream, you wrote this in your notebook. Add daily connecting affirmations around your big goal and living the dream in your head.

Finally, keep in mind that you may need to refocus your lens from time to time. Step back to ensure that you are not getting in your own way by including how and when requirements to your dream. When we start putting expectations on our dreams that tell the universe how to deliver your desire, we slow down the process. Allow the universe the opportunity to throw you the best surprise party ever. Stay out of the party planning. Be the guest of honor. Be prepared for the event by deciding, believing, and committing to the party, focusing only on the inevitability of the celebration.

There will be disappointments and setbacks along the way. These are simple affirmational speed bumps. These bumps in the road as you go over them will not feel good, but they will help you to refocus your lens as it will become even more clear, with each bump that this is what you want and there is nothing that is going to hold you back.

Expecting

Imagine that you are expecting some awesome package to be delivered to your house. This is a really important package, with high-value content. You receive notification that the package will arrive at your home between 10 a.m. and noon tomorrow. Just your luck, you have a meeting scheduled between 10 and 12 tomorrow that you can't get out of.

Of course, you don't want this high-value package sitting at your front door unattended, so you check with the neighbor to see if they will be home – no luck. You call around to family members and some friends and luck has it, someone is free to come to the house tomorrow between 10 and 12.

As soon as you get out of your meeting the next day, you call home. "Did the package arrive?"

"No, not yet," the person responds.

"But it should be there. Let me check the tracking or make a phone call and find out where it is."

You were expecting this package at a certain time, yet it didn't come. The package was valuable, so you took safeguards to make sure that it was received safely, but it didn't arrive as expected. Because it didn't arrive when it was supposed to arrive, does not mean that it won't still arrive. You state that you will follow up, because you still expect its inevitable delivery.

Your dreams are the same way. There will be times along your path that you believe, now is the time and you will be expecting, and something falls through. Your expectation of delivery, without prescribed timeframes and conditions must remain unwavering, even when what you think or want does not transpire.

There may be many resources for the universe to align, many people for you to meet, and connections to be made; these take time. Expectation without limitations and parameters provides the universe the freedom to give you exactly, if not more, that you dreamed when you are ready to receive it.

I can guarantee that the delivery of your dream will not be like the UPS or FedEx truck scheduled delivery. It's more like one day while eating lunch you realize that your dream is right in front of your eyes. There will be elements of your dream that begin to align, and you will recognize them, but the full fruition is usually subtle and just sort of slides into place.

For example, I had made a proclamation about a dream in relation to my company to a friend in March toward a very specific dream that I wanted to transpire by October. Now, I didn't set up my dream manifestation statements and affirmations with time constraints, but I made the comment to my friend and said that I was hoping for October. One day in October, I realized that my dream had indeed come true, but it had come true months earlier, and it took me months to recognize. It slipped right in. I had been living the dream that I had stated that I wanted to be living and I didn't even realize that it was so.

Often as we become laser focused on what we want and are regularly taking actions toward the manifestation of our desires, things are moving into place. I must tell you, this was not the first "surprise" dream manifestation realization. Years ago, I had been working toward a dream and a colleague asked me, "What is it exactly that you want? I'd like to add you to my prayer list." I immediately and succinctly provided him in just two words what I wanted. It was over a year and a half into living the dream, that not six months after telling him what it was that I wanted, I suddenly realized that EXACTLY what I had told him that I wanted, I received. And I must add, that when I realized what had happened, I immediately went to thank him profusely. I felt like he was a Buddha or something. It was such an intensely crazy realization that I got exactly what I asked for, and even though it was exactly what I had asked for it was so much better than what I even knew I wanted! A year and a half of living it and all of a sudden it hit me like a ton of bricks – this is what you asked for!

If you hold the expectation that you know that it is a matter of when, not if, it just seems to happen. We make it happen as we allow in the opportunity for everything to fall into place around us. And then one day, it hits you – HEY! How did this get here?! I have to admit, it will never get old, and now expecting is part of the fun. It's like that anticipation as a kid at Christmas wondering if that thing that you most wanted will be tied up with a big red bow under the tree. And even when it is not, you still look forward to the day it arrives with undying expectation that anytime, it can happen.

Affirming

In the focus step, I explained how daily affirmations will help you stay focused as you remind yourself through the visualizing and connecting process what it is that you desire. There is another piece to affirming your desires, and specifically, your big, audacious dream – Living Your Dream.

I have explained how during the affirmational visioning process that you will forge an emotional connection to how it will feel once you have your dream. Imagining how it feels to be driving through the Irish countryside, rather than simply stating, it will feel great to visit Ireland. Living your dream is not just an imaginary exercise, but starting now, I want you to recognize and provide affirmation for all of those things that you have right now that are a part of you living your dream experience.

In your journal, once a week you are going to write, "I am currently beginning to live my dream by…." At first this will be somewhat difficult, but it gets easier. I also believe that this is why I my dreams seem to slip in on me, because I am recognizing elements of them all the time, and acknowledging them.

One of the funniest ones for me is that used to say, "I don't want to wake up with an alarm clock." To me, even though I'm an early riser and a morning person, to be forced awake by an obnoxious alarm (even sweet, cute sounding alarms), just didn't resonate for me. A part of my dream life was to not wake up with an alarm.

I cannot tell you how many people that I would find myself saying, "It is so great to not wake up with an alarm. I am living my dream by not waking up with an alarm anymore." Yet I still didn't realize that my dream had come to fruition. It's okay, I eventually recognized its arrival and then set out to develop a bigger and more audacious dream!

Living your dream means that every single day you are guiding your destiny. *Destiny being the events that will necessarily happen to a person or a thing in the future, your fate.* Live your dream today as you guide the events. You are in charge here. If your dream is to be a millionaire, live your dream today. Will you be sitting with your feet kicked up on a Saturday morning enjoying a cup of coffee when you are a millionaire? If that is something that you enjoy now, can't you enjoy the same thing now that you will enjoy then? Sure, you may have a new home and be in a completely different environment, but there is nothing to stop you living like a millionaire now.

Would you be charitable? Volunteer your time as a millionaire? Why not now? Live your dreams now. You may not have the money to give, and even if you don't have time to physically go and help out, many organizations need really simple things, like helping out with social media postings. You can live your dreams now, and living your dreams provides one of the most powerful messages to the universe.

In the quantum world, you are a millionaire, and you are acting the part. There is no fake it until you make it. It's the authentic you, living your dreams today. Yes, you have expectations of an even grander experience and as you live it, it will get grander and grander. This dream is your property, you might as well be enjoying it now.

Think of it this way. Imagine yourself living in a tiny, dingy studio apartment and then one day you decided, I'm buying a house. You go out looking and low and behold, you find your dream home. It's in the perfect neighborhood, it's the right size and price, and you purchase it. You knew when you purchased the home that you wanted to remodel the bathrooms and the kitchen, but this is the perfect home for you.

You move in and over time you do the remodels. Even if you stayed in your dingy apartment while the remodels were being done, you'd be enjoying your property. You'd be picking out paint colors, and tile, and cabinets. You'd be purchasing furniture. You'd be taking steps in preparation of living in the completely remodeled house of your dreams. You would be participating in your dream daily. This is a firm action. Live your dream now.

Write down how you are living your dream. Every week as you write down how, in your dream notebook, say it aloud and then out loud state, "I am grateful to be living my dream." Let the universe know how happy you are to be living your dream now. This sets into action – like attracts like. The more joyous and grateful you are for what you have now, the more you will attract – and rapidly.

Receiving

Receiving, as I've stated, can happen without you being home waiting for the delivery person. It just sort of happens, but we must be open and willing to receive at any time. We also must set ourselves up to receive the unexpected.

What if one of your vision cards states that you desire to be your own boss. What if what you desire are the more literal elements of being your own boss? For example, you don't even realize what you really want is freedom. Ask yourself what activities can you think of that help you to feel free? Is there any activity that you could do today that would help you feel free? If physically unable – are you able to sit quietly and imagine yourself doing this activity in your mind? Perspective – think without limits and judgement of your current situation.

Begin living your what and why in your head and experiencing the feelings of receiving into your life the elements of your dream. Similar to the affirmational living of your dreams today, graciously receiving in your head the gifts from the universe, helps to usher in the delivery.

If today you were living your what, what would you need to do? The receiving element takes you into the future. Picture this like you just answered the door and were handed the package. What do you do next? You open the package, right? You unpack what's in the package. You read the instructions or assemble the contents. You begin using it. What does using it tomorrow look like?

Begin visualizing what your day would look like - the things that you would be doing or preparing for if your dream were here right now. If you were running a non-profit to feed the hungry, you would likely have a full calendar, networking. Why can't you begin finding out who you would need to know, now? Wouldn't it be helpful for later for you to know certain people or be familiar with certain organizations? Wouldn't it be helpful to know that you could be volunteering, if even from home after a full day of work, now, to prepare you for what it is that you would like to be doing?

This aligns with your affirmation, but take this one step farther, in your notebook, plan out the activities that you would need to do this week if your dream were fully manifested. As a millionaire, would you be planning a trip to the Caribbean? Write it down. Receiving – Planning a trip to the Caribbean.

Like I said, I didn't realize on many occasions that I had fully manifested many of my dreams until one day, I looked around and said, "Oh my gosh! I did it!" But the one thing that I make sure that I am always doing is planning for the future – setting up future deliveries by preparing to receive.

I receive consistently and I'm continually planning on what I am going to do when future deliveries arrive. When we do this, we keep the dream manifestation engine burning. We have it so fired up that it's a matter of churning out the next, re-developing visions for the future because bigger and better dreams than we could have ever imagined, just keep happening.

The Flow

Let me just say, with all of this planning and action, when you get in the flow, you will just know. You can feel when you are in complete alignment with the universe. You aren't stopping or blocking opportunity. You are just going with the flow – and it's a beautiful thing.

Dream manifestation pushes beyond positive thinking and applies consciousness and awareness of our thoughts, including those that don't serve us. We learn to interrupt negative thought patterns and replace them with beautiful and rich thoughts that support our belief in ourselves and our dreams.

Dream manifestation is embracing the creator in you, the mighty power in you to unleash infinite possibility into your life. Dream manifestation is recognizing that your purpose on this planet is to inquire and to seek knowledge through experience, to identify what you like and dislike.

Dream manifestation is the process of taking what you have learned that you desire and turn it into your reality. It is a means of taking a thought and creating something tangible. It is miraculous, and you are a miraculous creator.

Dream manifestation is your ordained birthright – welcome to the human race. Dream, love, and allow that beautiful energy to flow without interrupting the flow of others. Allow your energies to become synergistic and alive. Allow opportunities to explode and manifest into your life.

Seek, pursue, believe, and commit to your dreams. Don't let them go. Be gracious and confident in your ability and worthiness. You are a mighty creator, created in the image of God. You are meant to live the life of your dreams. You are meant to be limitless.

Flow with it and in it. Let the quantum energy of creation flow through you and about you. Be one with it. You are the artist. It's time to create and share your masterpiece with the world.

I wish you blessings of abundance as you create the life that you have always dreamed.

Namaste.

ABOUT THE AUTHORS

Dr. Jolene Church, Master Certified Success Coach, Keynote Speaker, Author

Personal Mission Statement

To encourage, inspire, and motivate people to see beyond the seen and believe that dreams can become reality- all in the context of joy, love, and excellence.

Dr. Church is the CEO and founder of Successful Thinking Mindset and Life Coach Training International She is a master certified success coach who helps individuals and organizations find success within. Her highly-regarded coach training certification program has helped prepare life coaches around the world to help people of all walks find success within.

Dr. Church's research in the area of critical thinking and decision-making of organizational leaders is at the forefront of transformational thinking. Dr. Church uses a time-tested thinking model to help her clients and audiences break down the barriers to their thinking to help them push through to new success.

An accomplished speaker, university professor, business leader, and author, Dr. Church has the ability to motivate and inspire her one-on-one coaching clients, corporate audiences, and readers to reach new heights; helping them transition to a better serving mindset - one that transforms impossible into possible.

Dr. Church's practical, down-to-earth teaching resonates with groups of all ages. She has a unique talent for helping others find their purpose, identifying their individual gifts, and defining their own personal success.

Dr. Church holds a Doctorate of Management in Organizational Leadership. Dr. Church has helped transform and turn-around troubled businesses for corporate giants Citibank and Bank of America as well as coached executives and individuals of start-ups, non-profits, corporations, municipal governments, and religious and academic institutions. Dr. Church's approach to helping people find solutions within has universal application.

With expertise in success psychology, personal development, organizational development, change management, organizational optimization, and transformation, Dr. Church uses these skills to re-program conditioned thinking into a successful thinking mindset.

Dr. Church's less than traditional background and backstory enables her to deliver meaningful and relevant content to her audiences as she breaks down the elements of personal and business success in such a highly energetic and engaging manner. She motivates her audiences to push past the status quo and embrace excellence as they break into their successful mindsets.

Darlene Trujillo Elliot, Life Coach, Lead LCTI Instructor, Author

Personal Mission Statement

To inspire, lift and provide resources for change and growth of individuals and organizations.

Life Coach, Darlene Trujillo Elliot is the lead instructor for Successful Thinking Mindset's Life Coach Training International and co-author of the soon to be released, *Dream Manifestation Live Your Dreams.*

Darlene is an avid community volunteer, logging more than 400 hours annually, leading many annual community events. Darlene serves as board member for TruEvolution and is the President for the Riverside Latino Network. Recently, she co-founded the Spanish Town Heritage foundation with a mission to champion Hispanic/Latino legacy by sharing the stories of the Southern California Inland Empire's first settlers, creating cultural learning opportunities, leading community efforts to restore and revitalize La Placita de Los Trujillo's, a place in history, learning, entertainment and the arts. The Riverside Tamale Festival is an event that benefits the foundation and takes place every year in April.

Darlene has received several awards for her community service. In March of 2015 she was selected as Latino Network's Celebración de la Mujer, this recognition is given to outstanding women who have demonstrated a spirit of commitment to their communities. May 2015 she was awarded Outstanding Community Service Award by the Allen Chapel AME Church, in Riverside. November of 2015 she was given the Greater Riverside Hispanic

Chamber of Commerce Josie Lozano Memorial Award for community service and political activism.

Darlene is a certified life coach and holds a B. A. in Organizational Leadership from Chapman University. Darlene has worked in local government for more than a decade and also sits on the State of California Podiatric Medical Board. Formerly Darlene was responsible for the City of Riverside Human Relations Commission (HRC), and Transportation Accountability Performance Task Force, the Mayor's Multicultural Forum. The HRC is a 15-member Charter commission with the task of creating an inclusive community. Recently, spearheading a LGBT+ Ad Hoc Committee with the main goal of bringing programs and services to the Riverside area, as well as brings awareness to the issues of the LGBT+ community.

ABOUT SUCCESSFUL THINKING MINDSET

Successful Thinking Mindset is a personal development and empowerment company designed to help people transform their lives and turn impossible into possible. We do this for individuals and for entire organizations. Whether you are in need of a business coach with more than 20 years' experience in strategy, transformation, and performance optimization or a personal success coach to help you get clear and focused and develop an action plan to get you to your goal - Successful Thinking Mindset is for you!

Successful Thinking Mindset is the Dream, Turned Reality for Dr. Jolene Church, Transformation Expert and Master Success Coach. Dr. Church has dedicated her life to helping people unleash their full potential by finding their "IT" and manifesting their dreams.

Let's face it, we don't all have hundreds and thousands of dollars to spend on workshops, seminars, or certification programs - yes, there are some that do - so that's why Successful Thinking Mindset is dedicated to offering products to help change the lives of as many people as possible with budgets to match all! Much of our content is absolutely FREE! From weekly blogs, to the podcast, and mini-coaching session newsletters (if you aren't on this list - you DO NOT want to miss out- you can sign up and www.successfulthinkingmindset.com).

Successful Thinking Mindset has its own publishing imprint so that we can bring to you, amazing, life-changing subjects for your personal growth!

Check out the other Successful Thinking titles available on Amazon:

It! Happens: A Practical Guide to Finding Your 'It' – by Jolene Church

Thinking 101: Fundamentals of a Successful Mindset – by Jolene E. Church and Brad Cotton

How to Write and Publish a Book in 30 Days – by Dr. Jolene Church

Success Coaching/Business Coaching

One of the best offerings from Successful Thinking Mindset is one-on-one coaching, with World Class Master Certified Success Coach, Dr. Jolene Church. Dr. Church has coached entertainment industry executives, CEO's, technology and Fortune 500 managers and executives, as well as front line workers, stay at home parents, and retired folks.

A people and business strategist, Dr. Church can help business owners, entrepreneurs, and executives align success between their organizations, their people, and systems.

You can find the coaching application form at the bottom of the Event Planners page at www.successfulthinkingmindset.com. - Yes - there is an application process, because we want to make sure that we are a good fit for you and what you are looking for in a coaching relationship!

Dr. Church only accepts a limited number of clients each month, but wants to make sure that those who might not be able to afford her coaching get a fair shake as well - that's why she gives away FREE coaching sessions every month! (See the blog page for the entry form).

For Businesses and Event Planners

- Successful Thinking Mindset Offers:
- Executive, Manager, Entrepreneur Success Coaching Sessions (Business Coaching/Personal Coaching)
- Performance coaching of your team or organization (individual or group)
- Customized employee and management training (emotional intelligence, performance, business strategy, communication, customer experience enhancement, team building, and more!)
- Success Coach Training for members of your organization (purpose/vision/goal achievement)
- Keynote (motivational/performance/team building/balance/purpose/excellence)
- (Check out the Contact & Bio page at www.successfulthinkingmindset.com for more information)

Life Coach Training International

Because we want to make sure that the mission of Successful Thinking Mindset founder, Dr. Church lives on,

To encourage, inspire, and motivate people to see beyond the seen and believe that dreams can become reality - all in the context of joy, love, and excellence,

Life Coach Training International was developed. This exclusive, premiere certification program is only offered by Successful Thinking Mindset and is only offered to a limited number of students each year, so that those who are a right fit for the program learn the exclusive Successful Thinking coaching tools to carry the torch and the mission into transforming lives of generations to come.

Dr. Church also offers an exclusive one-on-one Life Coach Training Program where she serves as your personal coach and mentor as you learn, practice and hone your craft, and build your business. (Check out the Life Coach Training International page at www.successfulthinkingmindset.com).

Successful Thinking Podcast

And how can we forget to mention the Successful Thinking Podcast?! - It's our newest product offering that is getting RAVE reviews! And it's FREE!!!! You can subscribe (again, no cost), on the Podcast page or through Apple iTunes or Google Play - just do it! These amazing episodes range from 20 minutes to an hour and are jammed packed with helpful "boundary breaking" tips to your greatest challenges. Oh ya! If you love our podcast - please help us out by leaving an iTunes review so that we show up higher in the search results for someone else (pay it forward folks)!

Something for EVERYONE and EVERY Budget at Successful Thinking Mindset. We are dedicated to helping break down the barriers in thinking around the world – so that people can obliterate those thoughts that aren't serving them and start living their dreams!

We thank you for becoming a part of the Successful Thinking Mindset Family!

Made in the USA
San Bernardino, CA
04 February 2019